COLLABORATIVE COGNITION

Recent Titles in
Advances in Discourse Processes

COLLABORATIVE COGNITION

Children Negotiating Ways of Knowing

David J. Bearison and Bruce Dorval

*with Gess LeBlanc, Andrea Sadow, Daniela Plesa,
and Commentary by Anna Stetsenko*

Advances in Discourse Processes
Roy O. Freedle, Series Editor

ABLEX PUBLISHING
Westport, Connecticut • London

KH

Library of Congress Cataloging-in-Publication Data

Bearison, David J.
Collaborative cognition : children negotiating ways of knowing / David J.
Bearison and Bruce Dorval.
    p. cm.—(Advances in discourse processes)
    Includes bibliographical references.
    ISBN 1-56750-657-7 (alk. paper)
    1. Cognition in children—Social aspects. 2. Cognition and
culture. I. Bearison, David J. II. Series.
BF723.C5C638 2002
155.4'13—dc21   2001045066

British Library Cataloguing in Publication Data is available.

Library of Congress Catalog Card Number: 2001045066
ISBN: 1-56750-657-7

First published in 2002

Ablex Publishing, 88 Post Road West, Westport, CT 06881
An imprint of Greenwood Publishing Group, Inc.
www.ablexbooks.com

Printed in the United States of America

The paper used in this book complies with the
Permanent Paper Standard issued by the National
Information Standards Organization (Z39.48–1984).

10 9 8 7 6 5 4 3 2

11/22/04

Contents

Contents

List of Illustrations

FIGURE

Acknowledgments

This research was supported by a grant to the first author from the National Institute of Child Health and Human Development (Grant No. HD27229). We gratefully acknowledge the assistance of Roger Bakeman who was a valued consultant on the sequential analyses of the data.

1

Social Cognition

There is growing interest today in the ways that social and cultural contexts constrain and promote children's cognitive development. Consequently, many studies of children's cognitive development have shifted their focus of inquiry from the individual child to the child interacting with others. From this stance, knowledge is not necessarily something that individuals possess or that evolves inside the head but rather something that individuals do together such that their social processes become intrinsic to their mental operations. According to Rogoff (1990), "the child and the social world are mutually involved to an extent that precludes regarding them as independently definable" (p. 28). The task then becomes to understand how children develop the interpersonal skills that enable them to negotiate the co-construction of knowledge. As will be seen, such a task can best be achieved when the interpersonal event is treated as the unit of inquiry and analysis.

A central component to studying socially contexted means of thinking is the role of culturally mediated forms of social interaction and ways by which interpersonal engagements foster children's cognitive development. This field of study has been informed, to varying extent, by the social dialogic features of the theories of Piaget (1950, 1967, 1995) and Vygotsky (1962, 1978) who, in turn, recognized Durkheim's (1925/1973) premise that logical operations developed socially. Although Piaget focused more on knowledge acquired laterally, and Vygotsky, vertically, both theorists recognized the social origins of cognition. By explaining how social interaction provides tools for children's cognitive development, they established methods for defining the social and cultural contexts in which it occurs (Bearison, 1986; Dorval, 1999). They share core assumptions regarding the social origins and collaborative features of cognitive development (Bearison, 1991; Chapman, 1989; Cole & Wertsch, 1996; Tryphon & Voneche, 1996; Tudge & Rogoff, 1989; van der Veer, 1996) along with many of the assumptions of self-regulating dynamic systems theories (Thelen & Smith, 1998). For example, according to Vygotsky (1987), Piaget did not ignore "the social factor as a determining force in the development of the child's thinking" (p. 82), and Piaget (1950) himself has argued that "it is precisely by a constant interchange of thought with others that we are able to decentralize ourselves . . . to coordinate internally relations deriving from different viewpoints" (p. 164). For Vygotsky (1978), "all higher functions originate as actual relations between human individuals" (p. 57).

Accordingly, we begin our discussion of the collaborative qualities of children's cognitive development with an assumption that all human activity, whether alone or in the company of others (i.e., on the intra- or interindividual plane), is socioculturally constrained, situated, self-regulative, and collective because of the culturally mediated means, artifacts, and tools (including language and speech) that are used to achieve some goal or purpose in activity. This assumption, however, does not carry with it implications of sociocentrism or any other forms of social reductionism. It does not, for example, consider knowledge and ways of knowing as communal activities that are prepackaged in cultural artifacts and that are acquired in ontogenesis without benefit of the interaction of biological and individual factors. The underlying psychological mechanism by which interpersonal relations are transformed to the intrapersonal, for Vygotsky (1978), constitutes an *internal reconstruction* of an external operation. This idea of internal reconstruction implies that the psychological mechanism is individualized in its function and not solely the product of social forces (Kitchener, 1996). Along these same lines, we reject a purely discourse-based kind of social constructivism which, according to Stetsenko and Arievitch (1997), "dissolves the self in the linguistic or social reality of discourse" (p. 159). Instead, we see the active co-construction of psychological activities as providing the basis to "conceive of the independent, agentic self without falling into the old pitfalls of dualism or reductionism" (Stetsenko & Arievitch, p. 169).

The antinomies reflecting multiple orientations of varying boundaries between the individual and the social, between the internal and external planes of knowing, and within which socially distributed activities account for individual cognitive development constitute some of the more exciting tensions and challenges arising in studies of social cognitive development today. The increasing tension between the individual and the social has become a target of productive criticism from many perspectives along the postpositivist and postmodern spectrum.

When considering the social context of knowing, the term "social" has been used to reflect two different, albeit related, aspects of the idea of a social context. One sense of the term refers to whether one or whether two or more individuals are participating in some cognitive activity. We use the terms "intraindividual" and "interindividual," respectively, to reflect the social context at this level of analysis. The other sense of the term "social" refers to the social situatedness of human activities that reflect mediational means that have been derived from cultural, historical, and institutional forces as well as the appropriation and use of both material and symbolic artifacts. We use the term "sociocultural" when recognizing this sense of social context.

Given these two senses of the term "social," a review of findings regarding questions about the social origins of children's cognitive development suggests that investigators ask fundamentally different kinds of questions depending on how they choose to operationally define "social." One group empirically assesses social influences by comparing children's interpersonal activities to their individual performances. Another group focuses its assessment more on the social context in which children work collaboratively. Which direction the researchers choose affects what sorts of cognitive activities are brought into the design of their studies and how they are used to discern the intentions, goals, beliefs, and perspectives of the participants. It also affects whether the investigator's unit of analysis is the individual or whether it is the social context of the interpersonal activity.

Along these lines, there have been two principal approaches in cognitive developmental psychology to studies of social interaction and cognitive change. One approach has been to observe various ways in which children interpersonally engage one another and then test how such engagements influence their cognitive functioning in solitary problem solving contexts. Although cognitive changes are attributed to the effects of children interacting, the unit of analysis in such studies remains the individual child. Another approach more clearly recognizes thinking as developing directly from socially and culturally mediated practices that provide opportunities for "culture and cognition to create each other" (Cole, 1981). In this approach, the unit of analysis, rather than being the individual as an independent entity, is some aspect of the social engagement that captures the social, cultural, and historical functions of conjoint activity within a problem solving system (Bakhtin, 1981; Leont'ev, 1981; Rogoff, Gauvain, & Ellis, 1984; Rogoff, 1998; Vygotsky, 1978; Wertsch, 1991).

According to both Piaget and Vygotsky, cognition, as an activity of social exchange, develops on both an interpsychological plane (in which social interaction leads development) and an intrapsychological plane (where the process and products of social exchanges become internalized and are available in subsequent interactions). In this way, children's understanding gained in collaboration with others incorporates social, cultural, and historical properties of knowledge and ways of knowing without the interpsychological (social) nor the intrapsychological (individual) planes of knowing necessarily being primary to the other or bounded by rigid criteria.

Because knowledge is mediated by a social system of knowing, it is experientially based and constructed and reconstructed at every level of individual development in activities that require children to make sense of situations in order to fulfill some culturally prescribed pragmatic purpose (Wartofsky, 1983). Development leads not only to more efficient means of constructing knowledge in sociocultural contexts but to knowledge that reflects increasingly higher levels of abstraction. This kind of development is culturally constrained and enabled by social activities in which participants negotiate with one another to sustain mutually derived goals or purposes. With development, such negotiations become increasingly dependent upon and reflected in children's ways of speaking (i.e., expressive language). Children's use of language (speech) as a means of mediating their social relations becomes a cultural tool to distance them from the immediacy of their pragmatic interests and means of achievement and, thereby, promotes development of abstract modes of reasoning and representing (Cocking & Renninger, 1993; Sigel, 1993). In collaborative practices then, the need to give voice to one's activities and to verbally critique another's has a necessary and powerful effect of distancing participants from the immediacy of the properties and consequences of their own activities and objects of cognitive inquiries (Damon, 1994; Verba, 1994).

Because the co-constructive qualities of children's cognitive development take place only when more than one child is present, research paradigms that single out one child for analysis preclude opportunities to observe the range of opportunities by which children acquire knowledge (Miller, 1994; Nelson, 1996).

How children develop by mastering the social cognitive tools of their culture explains how individual, social, historical, and cultural practices, rather than being independent entities, come to constitute each other (Vygotsky, 1962).

The focus of the present study, then, is on how children cognitively participate in social and cultural activities and less on the ways in which culture and society affect children's individual cognitive development. We do not claim that conversational discourse is the exclusive candidate with which to account for such participation. In addition to a range of non-verbal means of communicating, there is a range of motivational and emotional arousal factors that enter into the equation of collaborative cognition. However, our examination of children as interpersonal negotiators privileges the central role of language and oral discourse. Language, although a critical communicative tool, is also, via its semiotic functions, a basic cognitive tool that defines the parameters of what Nelson (1996) has referred to as the "emergence of the mediated mind." In this manner, language in discourse becomes constitutive of the realities upon which we cognitively operate rather than being simply expressive of prior discourse-independent realities. In other words, discourse serves not only an expressive function but also constitutes one of several kinds of cultural practices by which knowledge is co-constructed.

In the present study, we explored how knowledge and ways of knowing were generated in the dialogic discourse of children's collaborative activities—activities that required some level of mutual reciprocity in order for them to move forward in a systematic, organized, turn-taking sequence. This aspect of children's use of language in the joint construction of knowing corresponds to Bakhtin's (1986) account of speech genres (i.e., utterances that typically are tied to particular types of social situations) and the mediational means by which they shape and give meaning to communication and thought. Our goal in regard to understanding the emergence of speech genres in types of social situations marked by children's collaborative activities is to define and differentiate the course of its development.

PEER AND ADULT/CHILD COLLABORATION

In collaborative activities, there is the potential for contradictions to arise between a participant's initial perspective or way of constructing the meaning of an event and the perspectives of others. The ensuing need to verify and defend one's own perspective in coordination with other perspectives and relations has been shown to structure the process of interpersonal negotiations in ways that promote children's cognitive growth (Bearison, 1991). Furthermore, the felt obligation to reciprocally coordinate self/other perspectives is, for a variety of reasons, more likely to occur during peer collaborations than adult/child or expert/novice kinds of collaborative activities (Piaget, 1934). In other words, the active engagement of ideas between peers who are equal partners and who, therefore, do not need to defer to one another's intellectual authority, is thought to provide more fertile ground for the co-construction of knowledge than the guided participation of adults (or experts) working with children (or novices).

The distinction between these two forms of interacting—peers versus adult/child or expert/novice—is, in practice, more rooted in sociocultural contexts and in participants' culturally acquired and situationally specific modes of cognitive engagement than in any age or status differences between them. Thus, in some contexts, participants assume the role of the expert relative to a novice peer, whereas in other contexts, adults and children assume a more egalitarian form of reciprocity in their collaborations, and in still other contexts, the expert/novice roles between adults and peers can be reversed. Children's collaborative activities with peers of equal status, on the one hand, or with adults or children who have greater expertise, on the other, might best be understood as complementary resources in the development of their cognitive processes. Both domains call forth a level of shared understanding, or intersubjectivity, that have the potential to stretch the limits of children's knowledge.

Studies of peers collaborating typically are designed to tap different kinds of cognitive processes than studies of adult/child or expert/novice kinds of guided interactions, and, as a consequence, it is usually not possible to directly compare the effects of one sort of collaborative activity against the other (cf. Radziszewska & Rogoff, 1991). According to Damon 1991, "guided interactions [between adult and child or expert and novice] lead to the acquisition of practical skills, algorithms, and other 'modeling type' products of cultural transmission, whereas collaborative interactions [between peers] lead to the deep transformations of conceptual insight" (pp. 391–392). The former kinds of knowing refer to task-related tools derived from the context in which they are utilized, whereas the latter kinds refer to generalizable concepts across contexts. Consistent with this view, studies found that adults were better instructors of young children compared to peers when the task involved categorizing objects (Ellis & Rogoff, 1986) or memorizing explicit test items (Rogoff & Gauvain, 1986), but that children were more likely, in the company of their peers than of their mothers, to progress in moral reasoning, as well as to critique, clarify, elaborate, and transform each others' ideas, (Kruger & Tomasello, 1986; Kruger, 1992).

Another feature of the composition of collaborative groups concerns its size. Although collaborative activities occur among any number of participants, most studies of collaborative cognition have involved dyads because, as the size of a collaborative group under study increases, the methodological rigor with which the quality of the collaborative activities can be observed and measured decreases exponentially. This is particularly the case with studies, such as the present one, that rely on microanalytic dialogic analyses of interaction. How the qualities of children's interactions change as a function of increasing numbers of participants is not yet well understood (Rubin, Bukowski, & Parker, 1998).

SOCIOCOGNITIVE CONFLICT AND INTERSUBJECTIVITY

For Piaget, the activity of knowing, in its most fundamental sense, is regulated by a dialectic process of equilibration, disequilibration, and reequilibration. Disequilibration is seen as a perturbation to the knowing system, and it arises from different kinds of asymmetries in the evolving adaptation between individuals and their environments (Piaget, 1985). The process of resolving these types of perturbations follows the "logic of argumentation" (1985) and yields a higher level of cognitive development (i.e., reequilibration). Such perturbations or asymmetries have been referred to as cognitive conflicts when they occur on the intraindividual plane and as sociocognitive conflicts when they occur on the interindividual plane. In either plane, however, development occurs through the basic mechanism of conceptual conflict stemming from opposing centrations, and indeed, conflict, in one form or another, is a central motivating construct in most major theories of development (Chapman & McBride, 1992; Valsiner & Cairns, 1992).

According to Piaget's theory, because preoperational children lack the ability to decenter from the immediacy of their own perspectives, they are not likely to benefit from collaborative interactions with their peers. This has led some (e.g., Tudge & Rogoff, 1989) to question whether collaboration leads to the decentration necessary to benefit from peers interacting or whether a child's ability to decenter is a necessary prerequisite for collaboration to occur. For Piaget, however, the resolution of cognitive conflicts is ontogenetically first a social phenomenon because in social interactions contradictory centrations can arise simultaneously among participants, and, as Doise and Mugny (1984) have noted, these "cannot be as easily denied as a conflict re-

sulting from successive and alternating individual centrations"
(p. 28). Therefore, for Piaget, the key to the social foundation of
cognitive development is in the social origins of decentrations
since they arise from mutually conflicting interpersonal centrations that are more explicit, synchronous, and, hence, demanding
of verification and reconciliation in accordance with the principles of cognitive consistency, compared to conflicting intrapersonal centrations (Bearison, 1991).

The kinds of mental operations used to regulate and resolve
cognitive conflicts are the same whether the conflicts arise in-
traindividually in the course of solitary reflection or whether
they arise interindividually in the course of joint activities with
others (Piaget, 1950, 1971). Because the interchange of thought
with others in interactive contexts follows the same operatory
regulations as does intraindividual thought, interindividual interactions have the potential to reveal to experimental observation reasoning processes that are impenetrable, ineffable, or
simply not as readily apparent in solitary cognitive activities
(Bearison, 1982; Damon, 1983; Dorval, 1999). Hence, verbal interactions provide a more tractable mode of tackling the development of collaborative cognition.

This idea of fundamental isomorphisms between inter- and
intraindividual cognition also is reflected in Vygotsky's "general
genetic law of cultural development" in which intraindividual
cognitive functions retain the functions of social interaction:
"Any function in the child's cultural development appears twice,
or on two planes. First it appears on the social plane, and then
on the psychological plane. First it appears between people as
an interpsychological category, and then within the child as an
intrapsychological category. This is equally true with regard to
voluntary attention, logical memory, the formation of concepts,
and the development of volition. . . . Social relations or relations
among people genetically underlie all higher functions and their
relationships" (1981, p. 163).

Neo-Piagetians often use conflict to refer to discrepancies be-

tween one's own perspective and that of another in social interactions (i.e., sociocognitive conflicts). Vygotskian accounts of
social interactions, on the other hand, focus on asymmetric relations where the more and less expert come together. They observe how participants work together toward a shared definition
of a situation (i.e., intersubjectivity). In the present study, we
adopt a position that expands the notion of sociocognitive
conflicts beyond the clash of perspectives to a position that pre-
sumes that a struggle to establish conditions of mutual reciprocity is necessary in order for differing perspectives to be resolved
through negotiations that both maintain intersubjectivity and
promote new ways of knowing or making sense of a situation.
Hence, on the interindividual plane, the productive resolution of
sociocognitive conflicts can only occur in cooperative contexts of
interpersonal engagement in which participants are willing to
relax their individual constraints and acknowledge different perspectives and logically compare their value (Piaget, 1995). In this
regard, the term "conflict" has a meaning different from its col-
loquial usage and the resolution of a conflict is more than the
simple product of two individuals considering socially shared
alternatives. It represents a form of intersubjectivity based on the
joint comprehension of a topic achieved by the cooperative sharing of forms of reasoning (Rommetveit, 1976; Shantz, 1987;
Tudge & Rogoff, 1989). This conception of interpersonal conflicts
links the principles of dialectical development to social interaction (Csikszentmihalyi & Rathunde, 1998). This dialectic occurs
between people and cannot be attributed either to one individual
or the other in the discourse. Each participant accommodates his
or her perspective in order to assimilate that of the other person
and this process of social adaptation becomes the basis of direction, stability, and further growth (Wertsch, 1998). The discourse
components thought to be the expressive features of such kinds
of intersubjective conflicts include not only disagreements but
also agreements, questions, explanations, and compromise (Dimant & Bearison, 1991). In this way, the relative contributions of

participants in a dyad are emergent and transformative of each
others' ideas and ways of reasoning rather than being simply
additive and accumulative.

Language, a culturally mediated activity, is a mechanism by
which inter- and intraindividual functions emerge bidirection-
ally so that the developmental process is about both internalizing
the social and externalizing the individual, or, to state it more
correctly, the process can transcend such oppositional and unidirectional terms as "internalization" and "externalization." In
this regard, interindividual cognition offers a culturally constrained method of socially enacting previously realized intraindividual cognitive functions (Bruner & Bornstein, 1989; Nelson,
1996; Vygotsky, 1962). Consequently, the "sociocultural mind" is
as much a reflection of the "individual mind" as is its converse.
Hence, "it is as appropriate to assign to groups, as well as to
individuals, terms such as 'think,' 'attend,' and 'remember' "
when capturing the social origins of individual mental functioning (Wertsch, 1998, p. 111; Wertsch & Bivens, 1993).

RESEARCH DESIGNS

Individual and dyadic problem solving

Studies of the cognitive developmental effects of children's
collaborative activities with their peers have undergone a series
of design shifts since they were first introduced by "social Ge-
nevans" (Mugny & Doise, 1978). Extending earlier findings that
had shown that intraindividual conflicts can promote cognitive
development (e.g., Bearison, 1969; Inhelder, Sinclair, & Bovet,
1974; Smedslund, 1966), Mugny and Doise (1978) demonstrated
the cognitive consequence of children's dyadic interactions. Children collaborating with others (usually in dyads) in problem-
solving tasks were shown to solve problems at more advanced
levels than children working individually on the same problems,
and the differences typically were attributed to the cooperative
exchange of conflicting perspectives, or sociocognitive kinds of

conflicts, generated in the course of their interpersonal engagements (Mugny & Doise, 1978; Perret-Clermont, 1980). It also was found that children working together solved problems that neither child was able to solve alone (Doise & Mugny, 1984).

The now common design used to infer the effects of social interaction on cognitive growth consists of a pretest/interaction episode/posttest sequence with random assignment of participants to either individual or interaction problem-solving conditions during the interaction episode. In this design, confirmation of the facilitating effects of peer interaction relies on measures of individual cognitive functioning during the pretest and posttest sequences showing that pre- to posttest cognitive gain scores are greater among participants in interaction compared with individual problem-solving conditions. Using this design, some, but not all, investigators found that it was not necessary to pair children with more advanced partners for them to show individual improvement on the posttests (Dimant & Bearison, 1991), and that children who were paired with less advanced partners did not generally regress (Mugny & Doise, 1978). The most successful dyadic combinations were those in which children who functioned at intermediate levels of task mastery worked together (Mugny & Doise, 1978). Also, a substantial number of children in collaborative problem-solving situations used logical arguments and modes of reasoning on the posttests that were novel or different from those used in the pretests and to which they were not exposed during collective problem solving (Perret-Clermont, 1980; Weinstein & Bearison, 1984). It also was found that the cognitive effects of mutually reciprocal interactions, at least during the transition from pre- to concrete operational thinking, could not be achieved simply by allowing children to observe others interact in problem-solving contexts (Weinstein & Bearison, 1984). Taken together, these findings confirmed the cognitive effects of mutually reciprocal collaborative problem-solving activities—effects which could not be explained on the basis of unidirectional theories of learning or modeling.

However, findings across studies have not been consistent

when considered in terms of particular aspects of the quality of
peer relationships, the social context of the interaction, or the
task situation. For example, regarding peer relations, some studies found that sociocognitive conflicts were best generated when
children interacted with peers who were slightly, or just one
level, advanced in their cognitive reasoning (Azmitia, 1988;
Kuhn, 1972; Tudge, 1992; Tudge & Rogoff, 1989). Others found
that children collaborating with a partner equal in ability, or
even less advanced, also yielded cognitive gains (Forman &
Kraker, 1985; Glachan & Light, 1982; Light & Glachan, 1985;
Light, Littleton, Messer, & Joiner, 1994). Still others found evidence of cognitive regression when children were paired with
less advanced partners (Levin & Druyan, 1993; Tudge, 1992).
Several studies (e.g., Duran & Gauvain, 1993; LeBlanc & Bearison, 1997) found that it was not simply age differences between
partners that accounted for the cognitive gains of a younger participant collaborating with an older participant, but the quality
of the interaction engendered by the level of expertise that a
participant brought to the interaction, even if both participants
were matched on age. Other studies (e.g., Azmitia & Montgomery, 1993; Hartup, 1992) found that the affective valance of the
peer relationship (e.g., friendship status) made a difference in
whether or not children benefited from the interaction.

Observing dyadic interactions

Findings concerning the facilitating effects of dyadic interactions on children's cognitive reasoning abilities initially were
based solely on comparative measures of individual problem-
solving abilities before and after interaction. The theoretical relevance of sociocognitive conflicts was inferred from the pairing
of children of different or same initial ability levels and, because
the focus was on outcomes, collaboration was treated as a "black
box." However, investigators began to recognize that direct ob-
servations of children's interactions were necessary to assess the
kinds of interpersonal negotiations that facilitated development

and to explain why cognitive gains were sustained by some peer collaborators more than others. At the very least, observational evidence of participants' reciprocal engagement with each other's thinking was thought to be a necessary condition for advancing the argument that cognition is facilitated by collaborative activities among peers. Thus, a more direct test of sociocognitive conflict models of development emerged as investigators began to directly observe and systematically code the verbal discourse between participants.

Discourse coding schemes typically focused on the expression of different kinds of task-relevant disconfirmations and contradictions as behavioral markers of cognitive disequilibration. For example, Bearison, Magzamen, and Filardo (1986) found that dyadic interactions in which collaborators expressed task-relevant disagreements, contradictions, and contrary solutions in a balanced fashion were more effective in promoting individual cognitive gains than dyadic interactions that lacked these kinds of cognitive disconfirmations. Similar findings regarding the effects of sociocognitive conflicts on cognitive development were reported by Ames and Murray (1982), Berkowitz and Gibbs (1983), Emler and Valiant (1982), Light and Glachan (1985), Maitland and Goldman (1974), Miller and Brownell (1975), Peterson and Peterson (1990), and Walker (1983). However, others (Damon & Killen, 1982; Martin, 1985; Silverman & Geiringer, 1973; Tudge, 1985) found that the expression of disagreements during dyadic problem-solving activities among peers was not associated with individual cognitive gains. Damon and Killen (1982), for example, found that children who showed the greatest gains were more likely to both accept and "transform" their partners' statements than to contradict or disagree with them.

Interpersonal engagement

According to Rogoff (1998), there are critical, yet relatively unexplored, issues regarding the interpersonal dynamics of peer collaboration. In most of the literature in this field, peers have

been broadly and operationally defined as similar-age class-
mates. The assumption is that similar age equals equal status
among participants and that equal status generates the kinds of
social discourse that leads children, freely and cooperatively, to
examine the logic of arguments (both their own and their partners') that reciprocally advances their cognitive reasoning. However, even among children of similar age, equality of status may
be significantly compromised by a range of differences including
social status, situational expertise in a particular kind of cognitive problem, proclivities to control or take charge of collaborative activities, self-esteem and confidence in one's own abilities,
familiarity and comfort in interacting with the other, and a history of prior modes of interpersonal engagement in problem-
solving systems. Thus, across pairs of similar-age collaborators,
there is likely to be wide variation in styles of interpersonal engagement that affects the ways in which they work together
(Hawking, 1987; Verba & Winnykamen, 1992). Consequently,
there is a compelling need for research aimed at differentiating
which aspects of peer collaboration are most important in promoting partners' direct engagement with each other's thinking.

Although sociocognitive conflicts have been advanced as the
theoretical impetus for cognitive growth in collaborative activities, we are proposing a different form of conflict. It is derived
from the process of co-elaboration, whereby ideas are verbally
articulated for the communicative impact that they are intended
to have on the other in consideration of the other's differing
perspective or stance on a given topic of discourse and inquiry.
In other words, the felt need of participants to have to explain
their ideas so as to negotiate resolutions of interpersonal differences is a motivating force inherent in all forms of collaborative
activities. For example, Ellis, Klahr, and Siegler (1994) found that
successful collaborators clearly articulated their ideas and considered each other's proposals. They also found that proposals
that did not engage the interest of the other were likely to be
abandoned. Johnson and Johnson (1987) reviewed studies of cooperative learning and found a common component was that

learning was enhanced by having to explain one's ideas in consideration of another's perspective. According to Brown and Palincsar (1989), "change is more likely when one is required to explain, elaborate, or defend one's position to others, as well as to oneself; striving for an explanation often makes a learner integrate and elaborate knowledge in new ways" (p. 395).

Cognition in social interaction

The growing recognition of the need for participants to cooperatively engage one another if their collaborations were to advance cognitive change had the effect of expanding the cognitive components of peer collaboration beyond the disequilibrating effects of sociocognitive conflicts to encompass a broader range of interpersonal activities that, in turn, began to blur the conceptual boundaries between ways of interacting, on the one hand, and cognitive outcomes, on the other. Thus, earlier studies were seen as being predominantly "outcome" oriented. They used a pretest/interaction episode/posttest design in which children were randomly assigned to individual or collaborative problem-solving conditions. Later, this was expanded upon to include observational codes of particular features of peer interactions. More recent approaches, however, have shifted the design from "outcome" types of measures that reflected individual "in the head" types of attainments of concepts and skills to measures of how children's participation in collaborative activities (e.g., the management and transformation of interpersonal activities) serves as the basis of their cognitive development.

Accordingly, the essential components of peer collaborations are less likely to be associated with such individual characteristics as age, levels of expertise, or communicative competencies than with the kinds of social contexts that support opportunities for participants to collaborate with each other in a cooperative and mutually reciprocal fashion in the exchange and transformation of ideas (Crook, 1994). Rogoff (1998) captures the intersubjective qualities of such kinds of social contexts by treating development as "a transformation of participation of people engaged in shared endeavors. [This] avoids the idea that the social world is external to the individual and that development consists of acquiring knowledge and skills. Rather, a person develops through participation in an activity, changing to be involved in the situation at hand in ways that contribute both to the ongoing event and to the person's preparation for involvement in other similar events. Instead of studying a person's possession or acquisition of a capacity or a bit of knowledge, the focus is on people's active changes of understanding and involvement in dynamic activities in which they participate" (p. 690). In other words, the units of sociocultural analyses are the collaborative activities rather than their "outcome" in terms of some aspect of individual competencies, so that the process becomes the product, or, in other words, knowing becomes knowledge. In this way, the social dimension is not simply added on to what remains a fundamentally nonsocial cognitive model of development. In regard to applying these considerations to methods of inquiry in social cognition, we find that, although the pretest/ interaction episode/posttest design has done much to empirically advance the facilitating role of social interaction on children's cognitive development, as long as its effects are measured according to the achievements of individuals working alone, social influence is treated as somehow extrinsic to the individual's thinking. In order to advance a more intrinsic role to social interactions in individual development, we have adopted, along with others (e.g., Azmitia & Montgomery, 1993; Garvey, 1986; Gauvain & Rogoff, 1989; Hartup et al., 1993; Rogoff, 1990), a method of sociocultural analysis that is a more focused approach to participants' shared engagements in collaborative activities and which treats it as the basic unit of inquiry.

An example of such a kind of sociocultural analysis is a study by Dorval and Eckerman (1984) of developmental changes in the dynamics of participation among peers co-constructing free discourse in a study of interpersonal communication. They found that school-aged peers created conversations that increased in cognitive complexity with age. However, the increased complexity of their conversations was reflected less in *what* they talked about than in *how* they expressed the contents of their discourse. The latter reflected increasingly more complex modes of interpersonal coordination and expression of mutual intentions. Dorval and Gundy (1990) then examined the kinds of arguments that occurred in the same peer conversations. They found that the supposed clash of perspectives generated in arguing was less likely to affect cognitive levels of interpersonal coordination than levels of interpersonal coordination affected participants' modes of arguing.

The idea of cognition as a form of participatory collaboration in which there is a dynamic and irreducible tension between knowing and knowledge is supported by Werner's (1937) view of the relation between process and achievement in development. One of Werner's legacies was to shift meaning from achievement to process. Because different cognitive processes can lead to similar cognitive achievements and similar cognitive achievements can be the product of different kinds of processes, Werner maintained that achievement cannot be empirically dissociated from process. It is necessary, therefore, to empirically delineate at each step of a study how process and achievement are occasioned and to treat them analytically as interdependent lines of development, each giving form to the other. From such a perspective, the social component of children's cognitive development is not simply something that is added to what is fundamentally a nonsocial model of cognitive development but instead is understood as being transformative in the construction of knowledge and ways of knowing.

In sum, although early analyses in the field relied on individually administered measures of cognitive achievement to test the effects of social interaction, more recent approaches have shifted their focus from trying to establish the conditions for effective collaboration to trying to explain the role that these conditions play in mediating the emergence of collaborative cognition. The latter approach is a more socially contexted and process-oriented one in which the interactive context is the primary unit of analysis. These three historical approaches to the study of the cognitive effects of children's peer interaction and cognitive development parallel shifts in emphases between process and achievement (Werner, 1937) as summarized in Table 1.

Table 1
Paradigmatic Shifts in Studies of Peer Interaction and Cognitive Development According to How Process and Achievement Are Assessed

	Individual Pre-test	Dyadic Interaction	Individual Post-test
Phase I.	Achievement	Process inferred from pre- to post-test achievement change scores	Achievement
Phase II.	Achievement	Process observed and coded	Achievement
Phase III.		Process and achievement observed and coded as integrated, co-occurring lines of developmental change	

2

The Social Context of Interpersonal Negotiations

CHILDREN'S GAMES AS A COLLABORATIVE CONTEXT

The experimental tasks often used to test the effects of social interaction on children's cognitive development were derived from early Piagetian learning/training experiments (e.g., Inhelder, Sinclair, & Bovet, 1974). They consisted primarily of physical conservation problems, spatial coordination problems, and hypothetical moral dilemmas. Although children's search for collaborative solutions to these kinds of problems generated social discourse, it constrained a socially microgenetic process because the problems had a limited and finite set of solutions (usually in direct response to questions posed by the investigator) and the kinds of interactions that they generated were not necessary or intrinsic factors in the problem-solving context. That is, such kinds of problems could just as easily have been presented and solved individually as interactively. As will be discussed further, this limited the interactive context in regard to the potential for peer interactions to reveal theoretically significant features in the development of children's collaborative cognition. A principal aim of the present study, by comparison, was to achieve a more social-process-oriented approach to children's collaborative cognition with greater latitude both in the nature of the kind of task in which participants were asked to engage and the social context that the task engendered.

In keeping with the essential aim of our study to uncover patterns of collaborative discourse among peers that serve as means of negotiating task resolutions, we considered tasks that create social and cultural contexts that are more likely to allow participants to share control of topics of inquiry and discourse, in line with Vygotsky's (1978) idea that thoughts are constructed in the act of interpersonal communication. Thus, compared to the kinds of tasks used to create the social and cultural contexts of peer engagement in prior studies of cognitive change and peer interaction, we sought a task situation that both offered participants more leeway in regard to their ways of reasoning and justifying resolutions and was more consistent with children's everyday kinds of joint activities.

Bringing pairs of children together in order to co-construct their own kinds of board games is a social context that is, for a variety of reasons, a problem-solving situation with the potential to reveal process-sensitive features of peer interaction and interpersonal negotiations. In the present study, pairs of children were presented with a variety of boards and game materials and were invited to jointly create a board game they could play. A game was defined, for analytic purposes, as a series of rules regarding the use of selected materials intended to achieve mutually intended goals. First, because the number and kinds of game materials far exceeded what could functionally be incorporated into a single game, they created opportunities for the construction of a wide variety of games reflecting a range of goals, rules, markers, methods of advancement, and scoring. Second, because the activity was guided by "emergent goals" (Saxe, 1994) instead of a finite set of solutions to specific questions posed by an investigator, it was more fluid and open to interpersonal negotiations regarding a variety of goals, rules, and methods of play. As will be seen, this activity allowed for developmental analyses of relations between emergent sequences of interacting and co-constructing knowledge as it occurs both within dyadic collaborations (i.e., longitudinally) and between dyads (i.e., cross-sectionally). Third, because the activity took place in a practical mode of dyadic engagement, it captured the more routine, tacit, and immediate modes of engagement, compared to activities that occur in school-based problem-solving contexts, which typically are disassociated from the immediate context of their deployment (Scribner, 1985).

Rule-based play

How children interact when considering the constraining and enabling features of rules that define methods of playing board games provides a particularly rich sociocultural context in which to study collaborative cognition. Following Durkheim (1925/ 1973), rules are thought to function "both to regulate and integrate the social group—that is, to maintain its cohesion" (Nicolopoulou, 1993, p. 14). Rules, in this sense, are necessary components of the social structure of interpersonal engagement. According to both Piaget and Vygotsky, children's play involving rule-based board games is a leading activity and an essential prototype of their ability to recognize, comprehend, monitor, and coordinate self/other intentions in maintaining mutually derived goals and rules regarding cooperative behavior. Such kinds of play are a microcosm of their understanding of society because their sense of rules of interpersonal engagement captures the cognitive bases of relations that define the social contract between individuals and their society and culture (Habermas, 1984; Piaget, 1934, 1995; Vygotsky, 1978).

According to Piaget (1962), the transition from preoperational to concrete operational intelligence marks the beginning of a transition in children's preferences from pretend-type symbolic play to games that are social, competitive, goal oriented, and rule regulated. This transition in children's play follows from the increasingly reciprocal character of children's social relations as mediated by concrete operational thought. "As the symbol replaces practice as soon as thought appears, the rule replaces the symbol and integrates practice as soon as social relations are formed" (Piaget, 1962, p. 163). This is evident in the changing ways in which children understand the function of rules. During the preoperational period, children understand rules as being absolute and immutable. With development, they come to understand rules as malleable and relative to socially derived and mutually compatible principles of justice and fairness. The distinction between these two cognitive orientations about the regulative function of rules comprises the fundamental feature of social organization as it is codified in societal norms, institutions, values, and cultural belief systems.

Similar to Piaget, Vygotsky (1967, 1978) also recognized the developmental significance of the emergence of rules in children's play activities. For both Piaget and Vygotsky, this is nowhere more evident than in children's conscious realization of the function of rules in the construction of games. For Vygotsky (1978), games with rules are a "leading factor in development" (p. 101) because of their power to induce children to act against and/or delay their immediate impulses. "In this way a child's greatest achievements are possible in play, achievements that tomorrow will become her basic levels of real action and morality" (Vygotsky, 1978, p. 100).

During the first two years of life, make-believe or pretend play is exclusively solitary. It becomes increasingly more socially interactive from the latter part of the third year to about five to seven years (late preoperational to concrete operational periods). At this time, pretend play declines and is replaced by games with rules (Piaget, 1962; Rubin, Fein, & Vandenberg, 1983). Eiferman (1971) observed 1,400 children and found that pretend play declined from the third to the eighth grade while games with rules increased, achieving a peak at the fifth grade. Given this ontogeny of children's interest in and mastery of games with rules, participants for the present study were sampled from the first, third, and fifth grades (i.e., 6 through 10 years of age).

A sense of the kind of smooth and rapid flow of conversational turns that are generated in the collaborative discourse of participants co-constructing rule-based board games is provided in a verbatim excerpt from two fifth graders in Table 2.

CORRESPONDING DIMENSIONS OF DEVELOPMENTAL CHANGE: NEGOTIATIONS AND LEVELS OF GAME COMPLEXITY

Within the context of collaboratively constructing a game, we observed, coded, and analyzed two co-occurring and corresponding dimensions of developmental change. One dimension was interpersonal negotiations, which are the ways "by which one person tries to meet personal needs and goals in interaction, and often in conflict, with another person to whom he or she has some degree of positive ongoing attachment" (Selman & Schultz, 1988, p. 44). Negotiations consisted of two or more conversational turns between participants. They were coded according to how they reflected participants' ways of proposing, defending, justifying, and criticizing proposals about ways of enacting the game that they were co-constructing. Each conversational turn within a negotiation was coded according to its function so that we are able to define different negotiations by their sequence of conversational turn functions. Conversational turns within a negotiation are recursive in that each turn is both a reaction to the previous turn and an impetus for the next conversational turn. Recent advances in sequential analysis methods (e.g., Bakeman & Quera, 1995a) and the use of two-act sequence matrices (Eisenberg & Garvey, 1981) enabled us to measure the sequential co-occurrence of a variety of conversational turn codes and negotiations as they systematically changed across periods of discourse.

We also wanted to identify which kinds of negotiations were productive in terms of the cognitive complexity of the game as

Table 2
Verbatim Excerpt from the Collaborative Discourse of Two Fifth Graders (A & B) Co-constructing a Board Game

A: What kind of game do you want to make?
B: I have no idea.
A: Wanna use these cards?
B: Let's use the spinner.
A: Okay.
B: No dice, dice.
A: No let's use the spinner.
B: Right, because of the colors.
A: Yeah. And then um we can use these cards. No we don't need these cards.
B: No, not cards.
A: So we use
B: What's the object?
A: So we use the spinner, right. Oh, oh, I have an idea. Um, how many colors are there? 1, 2, 3, 4 (counts colors) Four colors, okay.
B: How 'bout you have to get the ladybug to
A: You have to get your ladybug to the middle, no, how 'bout
B: That's stupid.
A: No, that's too boring.
B: No but see, that's the point, but then you have, there's different ways

28

A: There's different obstacles, like say you have to go back or something. So, like if you go go like this (spins), oh we can use the die too. Because you each, we each have a ladybug, okay. And then we have to roll.

B: Oh I know, I know. You spin, okay?

A: Yeah.

B: You spin and you roll.

A: Yeah.

B: Whatever color

A: How 'bout we each have two, one ladybug

B: Gold is go again. Cause you want to get to the gold.

A: One pig.

B: So like let's say I end up on blue,

A: Mmm hmm.

B: I move to blue and then I have to roll the dice.

A: Oh no how how bout this. You, you um roll the dice, right. And, no wait, wait.

B: Ooh, you roll the dice and let's say I got seven. 1, 2, 3, 4, 5, 6, 7, yellow. So now I have to try and get yellow.

A: And if you get yellow then you get to move an extra point.

B: Right.

A: Okay, so like, okay, so you roll the dice.

B: We should use one die cause otherwise it's gonna be over too soon.

A: Oh yeah that's right. So you roll the dice. The number that you get, you move up and then you try and get that number on there. If you get that number, you wanna use the money?

29

Table 2 (*Continued*)

B: Okay.

A: We have to get, how 'bout we need two ladybugs, I mean, one ladybug.

B: We each have a ladybug and a pig.

A: Yeah. And

B: And like Sorry, you can choose which one to move. But no obstacles.

A: Yeah.

B: Just like you choose which one to move.

A: How 'bout, how 'bout we should have like lose one turn, cause then it will be easy.

B: If you get, if you spin a gold, if you spin and it lands on gold, then you have to move back two spaces.

A: Okay.

B: And that's the only obstacle. Come on. Let's just try it that way and we will see.

A: Okay.

it was being jointly constructed. Hence, the other developmental dimension was the contents of the game (i.e., the nature of its rules, goals, and procedures). Here we were concerned with how the game reflected the abstract logic (according to ways by which the game contents were differentiated and hierarchically integrated) of the participants' activity as it continued to evolve with each negotiation.

This idea of correspondence between two dimensions of development rested on the assumption that the nature of a game so constructed sprang not from the personal striving of an individual participant, or even from one participant adding to the contribution of the other in a dyad, but from the nature of the interaction between participants. Their co-constructions, therefore, were understood to be transformative rather than simply additive or accumulative. In the vernacular of structure/function relations, levels of game complexity reflect joint knowledge that can be construed as the structure of the collaborative activities, and participants' ways of negotiating reflect ways of knowing that serve as the function. Together, the assessment of structure with respect to function can be expected to yield patterns of developmental change (Kaplan, 1974). In the present study, the function of interpersonally negotiating proposals for co-constructing board games yield structurally more complex kinds of games.

COORDINATING PERSPECTIVES

As Wertsch (1998) has pointed out in his discussion of culturally mediated activities in sociocultural research, "one of the potential dangers of sociocultural research is social reductionism, or the assumption that it is possible to reduce accounts of human action to social forces alone" (p. 141). Even for Vygotsky, "any new form of cultural experience does not simply come from the outside, independently of the state of the organism at a given point in development" (Wertsch, 1979, p. 69). Hence, it is necessary to recognize the tension between agent and culturally me-

diated means in studies of collaborative cognition by acknowledging where children are in their cognitive development
so that explanations about the quality of their interactions is not
reduced simply to their sociocultural milieu.

The situated components of our analysis of children's collaborative cognition call for a measure of their sociocognitive status
that is more socially derived than simply that which is afforded
either by the use of age as a marker of their development or a
global measure of their intelligence. Because the qualities of children's peer interactions theoretically are derived from their ability to coordinate self/other perspectives (i.e., social adaptation),
an appropriate indicator should similarly reflect their understanding of their partners' thoughts and feelings relative to their
own. Selman (1980) has provided such a measure. He has identified five stages of reflective perspective coordination within
four different interpersonal domains by categorically coding children's responses to questions about the resolution of a series of
interpersonal social dilemmas. Of these four domains, dilemmas
and questions concerning the nature of friendship were used to
access perspective coordination in the present study because, according to Selman, they specifically deal with the "resolution of
discord and conflict between two individuals" (p. 106) and, thus,
most closely capture the underlying issues in children's negotiations employed in the context of co-constructing a rule-based
board game.

Selman's stages of perspective coordination begin with an egocentric level where others are not understood as having perspectives different from one's own and culminating at a stage
where several perspectives that transcend that of the individual
are coordinated. At Level 0, "there is no clear differentiation between the social or intentional perspectives of self and others. At
subsequent levels of reflection the child comprehends that another person's subjective thoughts, feelings, and intentions are
distinct from the self's (early childhood: Level 1); that the other
person can reflect upon and consider as distinct the self's subjective attitudes, feelings, and motives (middle childhood: Level

2); that the self and other can view self's and other's psychological points of view mutually and simultaneously (preadolescence: Level 3); and that there is a more general social viewpoint that transcends individual perspectives and involves a mutual understanding of deeper psychic processes within and between persons (adolescence and adulthood: Level 4)" (Selman & Schultz, 1988, p. 384). These stages form an invariant sequence that are qualitatively different and hierarchically organized. In addition to its firm conceptual base, Selman's measure has high test-retest and inter-coder reliability. Selman and Jaquette (1977) reported inter-rater reliabilities between 94 and 97%. Pearson correlations for test-retest reliability for second and third graders across a two-month and five-month period was 0.61 and 0.63, respectively (Cooney, 1977) and for fifth- and sixth-graders across a 5.5-month period, it was 0.92 (Enright, 1976). Within the age range of 5 to 14 years, Selman reported a steady linear development of mean scores for interpersonal understanding.

JOINT PLANNING

Pilot research had shown that, in the present context involving the joint construction of a board game, all participants went through an initial period of interacting in which they negotiated some of the rules and methods of playing the game before attempting to enact the game that they were co-constructing. Also, after initiating a game enactment, it was possible for participants to step out of the context of playing the game in order to negotiate further game proposals. These kinds of negotiations, occurring outside of game enactments, were thought to reflect a particular kind of metacognitive skill involved in the development of children's planning behaviors. According to Pea (1982), "Planning is a complex form of symbolic action that consists of consciously preconceiving a sequence of actions that will be sufficient for achieving a goal. It is set apart from undeliberated action, which is not preconceived" (p. 6) and, hence, lacks metacognitive skills. Interest in children's planning activities has been guided by increasing recognition of metacognition as an integral aspect of higher mental functions (e.g., Flavell, 1977; Leont'ev, 1981). Hartup (1985) suggested that metacognitive skills, like planning, are especially likely to benefit from social interactions because the need to verbally communicate to a partner preconceived intentions about methods of playing the game encourages participants to give more thought in advance to what they need in order to coordinate their own and their partner's activities. Consistent with findings from Gauvain and Rogoff (1989), it was expected that older children or children capable of constructing more complex kinds of board games would be more likely to plan prior to initiating their enactment of the game they were co-constructing.

GENDER DIFFERENCES

Studies of dyadic peer interaction consistently have maintained same-gender dyad compositions. Although most studies have not reported nor tested for gender differences, many investigators found unexpected gender differences. Bearison, Magzamen, and Filardo (1986), for example, found that male dyads produced more kinds of interactions that were associated with cognitive gains than female dyads, so that, although there were no gender differences on the preinteraction achievement measures, males had significantly higher scores on the postinteraction measures. Nisan (1976) found that collective, compared to individual, deliberations among boys, but not girls, resulted in developmentally more mature decisions to delay gratification. Tudge (1985) also found significant gender differences in favor of social interactions for boys on mastery of Siegler's (1981) balance beam problems. Hartup et al. (1993) found that girls were more likely than boys to justify their assertions during peer discourse and Miller, Danaher, and Forbes (1986) reported greater "conflict mitigation" among girls and more threats and force among boys. Similarly, Sachs (1987) and Sheldon (1990) found that girls made greater efforts in discourse than boys to maintain the interaction. Ellis and Gauvain (1992) found that "When interacting in same sex groups, boys tend to talk longer and more frequently, interrupt more, attempt to 'top' another's story, provide information, and exert control over the topic of conversation more than girls, whereas girls simultaneously attempt to gain their own way and sustain the interaction by agreeing with points others have made, pausing to give others a chance to speak, and offering gentle directions, as opposed to commands, to their partners" (p. 163). Also, peer interaction studies with more than two participants in mixed gender groups found gender differences in school-related academic activities (Lindow & Wilkinson, 1985; Webb, 1984; Wilkinson & Marrett, 1985). These findings raise basic questions regarding the extent to which these kinds of gender-related patterns of discourse and patterns of interacting are specific to particular types of situated social interactions. Therefore, the present study tested for gender effects although there was no theoretical basis to expect them (Caplan, Crawford, Hyde & Richardson, 1997).

RESEARCH QUESTIONS ABOUT NEGOTIATIONS

Consistent with the nature and function of negotiations in conversational discourse, we were interested in those aspects of discourse when a participant proposed and managed information about methods of game playing that were inconsistent with or contradicted their partner's ideas about constructing the game. Such conditions called forth some manner of negotiation between participants, the observation of which led us to the following kinds of research questions:

- How are different kinds of negotiations constructed by sequences of conversational turns?
- How do the conversational turn sequences in negotiations qualitatively change during the course of social interac-

tion as partners become more familiar with each other
and with the social context in which they are participating?

- Do the kinds of negotiations and/or the level of complexity of children's game constructions change as a developmental function of their joint ability to coordinate
self-other perspectives?

- Is the quality of children's negotiations and/or their game
constructions associated with their gender or grade level?

- How are different kinds of negotiations longitudinally related to the evolving complexity of children's game co-
constructions?

- How are different kinds of negotiations cross-sectionally
related between dyads to the evolving complexity of children's game co-constructions between dyads?

- What conversational properties of negotiating sequentially map onto changes in evolving levels of game complexity?

- Are children's propensities to plan their joint game activities prior to enacting them in the course of playing the
game they are constructing related to levels of game complexity?

- How is the relative balance or mutual synchrony between
partners' ways of contributing to interpersonal discourse
related to the quality of their negotiations and the complexity of their game constructions?

3

Method

PARTICIPANTS

Participants were 180 children, 60 each from grades one (M age = 6 yrs., 6 mos.), three (M age = 8 yrs., 9 mos.), and five (M age = 10 yrs., 4 mos.) from six schools in a large urban city. Participants were recruited from among all children in given grades and schools whose parents gave informed consent. Consent also was obtained from each participant. The children's ethnic backgrounds were as follows: 51% Caucasian, 29% African American, 12% Asian, 7% Latino, and 1% American Indian.

Within a given school and classroom, participants were randomly assigned to same gender dyads. The only constraint on the randomization was that teachers reviewed the names of paired children and identified any pairings of children who were either "best friends" or who obviously did not get along with each other. In those few cases, changes were made to eliminate such types of pairings.

PROCEDURES

Dyadic measures were derived from sets of interaction codes of (1) conversational turns, (2) negotiations, and (3) collaborative game constructions. In addition, an individual measure of participants' perspective coordination abilities was obtained as an index of their level of social cognitive development. However, in the analyses, participants' levels of social cognitive development were entered as dyadic mean scores so as to preserve a dyadic unit of analysis.

Individual developmental level

Participants met individually with an examiner in a separate room in their respective schools. They were read the children's version of "The Friends Dilemma" from Selman's (1980) interpersonal understanding interview. This dilemma is about a child who has to make a choice between honoring a previous engagement with his or her longstanding "best friend" or attending a special and prized event with a new friend. The names of the children in the story were matched with the participants' gender. After being read the story, participants were asked 11 open-ended questions (Selman, 1980) designed to elicit levels of interpersonal perspective coordination.

Responses to each of the 11 questions were scored according to Selman's (1980) criteria for level of perspective coordination: Level 0: Undifferentiated and egocentric perspective taking; Level 1: Differentiated and subjective perspective taking; Level 2: Self-reflective/second-person and reciprocal perspective taking; Level 3: Third-person and mutual perspective taking; Level 4: In depth and societal-symbolic perspective taking. The range of scores for each participant was 0 to 44.

Dyadic interaction

To avoid having the Selman perspective coordination task influence game construction activities, no less than 4 weeks after the administration of the perspective coordination task, pairs of participants (dyads) were brought to a separate room in the school equipped with a small table, chairs, and video recording equipment. For the initial five minutes, dyads were simply asked to talk among themselves while the experimenter left the room, ostensibly to check whether the recording equipment was functioning properly. This phase of the interaction was not scored for present purposes. After five minutes, the experimenter returned and placed the following game materials on the table:

A square board, 18 by 18 inches, with five equidistant square rows of circles, each row bearing a different set of colors (grey, green blue, red, gold, and yellow) and with consecutively smaller numbers of circles (from nine at the perimeter to one in the center).

A circular board, 18 inches in diameter, with five identical bands emanating equidistantly from the center (marked by a gold circle). Within each band were 11 concentric rings of different colors (green blue, red, and yellow) across the bands. In addition, there was a band at the periphery of the circle with 16 grey rings and another band halfway between the periphery and the center with 8 grey rings.

16 rubber animals, .75 inches tall, of 4 different species: 4 dogs, 4 pigs, 4 lady bugs, and 4 fish

25 plastic pawn-shaped pieces: 5 each of blue, green purple, white, and red

2 numbered die

a colored cube, .5 inches, with blue, yellow, gold, grey, green, and red on each side

12 plastic chips, 4 each of red, yellow, and blue

10 cards, each with a number from 0 to 9 on its face

piles of paper money in denominations of $5,000, $1,000, $500, $100, $50, and $10

a 3 × 5 inch pad of paper

a pencil

a round spinner, 8 inches in diameter, with 12 pie-shaped divisions with the following two matching colors at opposite divisions: gold, brown, red, green, yellow, and blue

2 2.5 inch-tall plastic robots

The game boards and game materials were designed and produced by artists especially for use in the present study so that, although similar in many respects to materials from commercially produced board games, they did not suggest (according to pilot testing) any particular board games with which participants might already have been familiar.

Participants were then told the following: "Look at all these different things you can use to make up a game. I'd like you to make up a game together so you can play it. Just choose one of the game boards, and then you can use whatever other stuff you want." The experimenter then moved out of the dyads' sight and allowed the interaction to proceed for 25 minutes.

Dyadic sessions were videotaped with a camera and built-in microphone on a tripod placed five feet from the front of the table. All participants were told that they were being video-recorded. The audio portions of the videotapes were transferred to audiotapes. The audiotapes were then transcribed, and the transcriptions were then checked against the corresponding videotapes for clarification and corrections. In places where participants made ambiguous verbal references to certain game activities or materials (e.g., by using indistinct pronouns along with gestures), or where gestures alone where used, the correct references were obtained from the videotapes and added in parentheses to the transcripts. The transcripts consisted of a series of negotiations composed of two or more conversational turns between members of a dyad. A conversational turn began when a speaker began talking and ended when he or she stopped talking (excluding interruptions by the other speaker, unless the current speaker explicitly responded to the interruption).

CODING INTERACTIONS

The basic unit of analysis was a negotiation consisting of two or more conversational turns. The start of a negotiation was marked by the initiation of a proposal regarding procedures of play, uses of materials, or changes in existing procedures or uses of materials. A negotiation continued through successive conversational turns, back and forth, between partners until the initial proposal and its derivatives were no longer the topic of discourse. Two or more conversational turns constituted a negotiation, where the initial turn typically was an initial proposal (but also could have been an elicitation for a proposal). An exception was that there would only be a single conversational turn in a negotiation when a partner indicated acceptance of an initial proposal by the use of a nonverbal gesture.

An outline of the nine sets of dyadic interaction codes are presented in Table 3 and are described as follows:

I. CONVERSATIONAL TURNS

A. Functions

The first set of codes defined the function of the conversational turns that collectively constituted a negotiation. Conversational turns, back and fourth between partners, provided a means for statistically defining different kinds of negotiations according to both their frequency of usage and their sequential patterns of occurrence. There were 13 mutually exclusive and exhaustive conversational turn codes:

Initial proposal—a statement describing a generalized method of play or a goal for playing. An example: "Let's place the red chip over here."

Counterproposal—a disagreement with a preceding proposal within the negotiation, together with a substitute proposal. An example:

Table 3
Outline of Dyadic Interaction Codes

I. Conversational turns

A. Functions
   1. initial proposal
   2. counter proposal
   3. disagreement
   4. agreement
   5. elicitation
   6. repetition
   7. demonstration
   8. elaboration
   9. qualification
   10. compromise
   11. confirmation request
   12. ignore or an aside
   13. clarification

B. Justifications
   1. Unjustified
   2. Factually justified
   3. Perspectively justified

II. Negotiation Episodes

A. Types of Negotiation Strategies
   1. Ignored
   2. Unresolved
   3. Withdrawn
   4. Acquiescence
   5. Acceptance of proposal
   6. Expansive
   7. Compromise
   8. Synthesis

B. Game Topics
   1. Designation Rules
   2. Procedural Rules
   3. Conditional Rules
   4. Constraining Rules
   5. Goals

C. Joint Planning
   1. Planning
   2. Active

42

III. Game Complexity Components

A. Change Indicators
   0. No change
   1. Change up
   2. Change down

B. Change Components
   0. No change
   1. First designation or procedural rule
   2. First conditional rule
   3. First explicit goal
   4. First system of scoring
   5. First additional goal
   6. Every constraining rule
   7. Every complex conditional rule
   8. Every rule for alternative pathway
   9. Every goal for alternative pathway

C. Backward Pathway
   0. No
   1. Yes

D. Evolving Levels of Complexity
   Continuing sequence of numbers of
   complexity levels

43

A: "It's the dogs that get to start."

B: "No, the robot gets to start."

(In this and the following examples, when two or more conversational turns are presented [i.e., (A), (B), (A) ...], the last turn gets the exemplary code).

Disagreement—a disagreement with a previously expressed proposal within the negotiation or with the partner's statement or enactment in the immediately previous turn. An example: (A) "If you spin gold once, you get a fish." (B) "No, we shouldn't use those guys."

Agreement—an agreement with a previously expressed proposal within the negotiation (either expressed verbally and/or enacted by gesture [e.g. shaking head affirmatively]). An example: "OK, go ahead."

Elicitation—a request for further information about a proposal. An example: "Well, what's this for?"

Repetition—a repetition, although not necessarily literal, of a previously expressed proposal, counterproposal, demonstration, elaboration, qualification, or compromise within the negotiation. An example: (A) "That's your ten. You're the banker." (B) "No, no, you give me all the rest of the money over there." (A) "Yeah, but you're the banker."

Demonstration—a presentation of how a proposal would function. An example: "I can go wherever I want. You can go like that or like that. You can go 1, 2, 3, 4, 5 [demonstrates movement of marker on the board]."

Elaboration—a partner augments the other's proposal about the conditions of the game being constructed. An example: (A) "When we play, we go like this. You start from here and I'll start from here and ..." (B) "And whoever gets to this first, wins. Yeah."

Qualification—a restriction or constraint on the conditions of deployment on the partner's or the self's previously expressed proposal. An example: (A) "You're going to eat a bug, right?" (B) "Only if I get a red."

Compromise—a suggestion by one partner of a way to reconcile a disagreement about a proposal by integrating aspects of the opposing position. An example: (A) "OK, I'll be these two robots." (B) "I'll be these four dogs and my dogs, are over here." (A) "You can only get two things at a time cause there are only two robots to play with." (B) "OK then, you get to choose two more things to be."

Confirmation request—a question by one partner concerning whether the other partner agreed with his or her statement. An example: "So, do you agree with that?"

Ignore or an aside—one or more statements by one partner that were nonresponsive to the other partner's proposal (or elicitation). An example: (A) "Let's move the robot to the center, if you get a blue." (B) "Look, it's snowing outside."

Clarification—an explanation offered by one partner regarding the meaning of a proposal that did not alter (or expand) its conditions of deployment. An example: (A) "Yellow is worth the most." (B) "Yeah, why?" (A) "Because there's a few blacks and less yellows."

B. Justifications

Conversational turns also were coded for whether or not they were justified. It was expected that conversational turns that were justified, compared to unjustified turns, would be associated with several indicators of discourse and game level complexity. There were three mutually exclusive and exhaustive justification codes:

Unjustified—Conversational turns stated without any justification

Factually justified—Conversational turns justified in terms of the methods of play. An example: "No, it's not. Well, not really. I don't think we should, because that's not like the object of the game."

Perspectively justified—Conversational turns justified in terms of self and/or other's perspective (i.e., thoughts, feelings, intentions, or behavior). An example: "No, George. You can't make up all the rules."

II. NEGOTIATIONS

Negotiations were coded for three dimensions: (1) the kind of negotiation in terms of proposals regarding methods of play (rules and goals), (2) the topic of the proposal, and (3) whether they took place during the course of playing a game or during time off from playing a game.

A. Kinds of negotiations

There were eight mutually exclusive and exhaustive kinds of negotiations. They varied according to levels of discourse complexity which were expected to be associated with levels of game complexity.

The two developmentally most complex kinds of negotiations, compromise and synthesis, were thought to involve a level of formal operations on abstract representations and, hence, to be largely beyond the cognitive competencies of the present participants. They were included in order to test this proposition and also to see whether such kinds of negotiations might be achieved in reference to solely concrete representations of joint game construction.

Ignored—One partner changed the topic of discourse without responding to or recognizing one or more proposals offered by the other partner. An example:

A: "Let's use the red ones." (*initial proposal*)

B: "Whoever gets on the gold, goes first." (*ignore*)

Unresolved—One partner changed the topic of discourse without reconciling one or more contested proposals. An example:

A: "Let's use the red ones." (*initial proposal*)

B: "No, that's stupid. I want to use the green ones." (*counterproposal*)

A: "Whoever gets on the gold, goes first." (*counterproposal*)

Withdrawn—One partner withdrew his or her proposal without a counter- or compromise proposal in reaction to objections expressed by the other partner. An example:

A: "Let's use the red ones." (*initial proposal*)

B: "No, that's stupid." (*disagreement*)

A: "Oh, all right then." (*agreement*)

Acquiescence—One partner passively accepted the other's proposal (without elaboration) by expressing something like, "Yeah," or "OK," or by enacting the proposal at the next turn. An example:

A: "Let's use the red ones." (*initial proposal*)

B: "OK." (*agreement*)

Acceptance—One partner accepted the other's proposal after actively considering it in the form of either an unacceptable proposal, a counterproposal, a repetition, a disagreement, or a verification. An example with a counterproposal:

A: "Let's use the red ones." (*initial proposal*)

B: "No, that's stupid. I want to use the green ones." (*counterproposal*)

A: "But the green ones don't fit in here." (*disagreement*)

B: "Oh yeah, you're right." (*agreement*)

Expansive—One partner accepted the other's proposal but only after having added new conditions to it or having offered a counterproposal that was unconditionally accepted by the other. An example is:

A: "We'll use the dice and move whatever spaces the number is." (*initial proposal*)

B: "Yeah, and if you get a six you get an extra turn." (*elaboration*)

A: "Hey, that's a good idea." (*agreement*)

Compromise—One partner adjusted the other partner's proposal by incorporating the conflicting claims or disagreements that he or she had with the other's proposal (i.e., a settlement of differences by mutual concessions). An example:

A: "We'll use the dice and move whatever spaces the number is." (*initial proposal*)

B: "Yeah, but if you get a six, you lose your turn." (*qualification*)

A: "No, you should just go as many (spaces) as the dice tells you." (*repetition*)

B: "Well then, what if you lose your turn if you land on a red space?" (*compromise*)

A: "Yeah, that'll work!" (*agreement*)

Synthesis—One partner resolved differences between his or her own proposal and the other's proposal by incorporating or logically integrating aspects of each of their preceding and conflicting proposals. An example:

A: "Whoever gets to the center first wins the game." (*initial proposal*)

B: "No, whoever goes all around the outside of the board first wins." (*counterproposal*)

A: "That's dumb because the prize has to go in the center." (*disagreement*)

B: "OK, then you first have to go around the outside of the board before you can move to the center, and the first person who gets there, wins." (*compromise*)

A: "Yeah, I like that!" (*agreement*)

B. Game topics

The game topics referred to the purpose of the negotiated proposals as they established new rules or goals or affected existing ones. Rules referred to methods of play (the "how" of playing) and goals, to the purpose or object of play (the "why" of playing). Game topic codes were exhaustive but not mutually exclusive. That is, a negotiation could be coded for more than one game topic. Game topics were used to code the evolving complexity of the games partners were co-constructing. There were five game topics:

Designation rules—indicated labels of pieces, values attributed to pieces, and their places on the board. An example: "This is the place where we keep the money."

Procedural rules—designated procedures or methods of play (in terms of moving pieces on the board). An example: "You have to roll the dice to see how far you get to go."

Conditional rules—implied or stated "if then" relationships between game conditions and procedures of play. An example: "If you get to the blue, then you get five dollars."

Constraining rules—created parameters of play (i.e., boundaries or constraints) that did not exist before and within which other preexisting rules must now operate. An example: "If you get anything besides green, you have to go there until you get a green."

Goals (and subgoals)—designated the object or purpose of the game or, in the case of subgoals, some part of the game. An example: "The first one to get to the center wins."

C. Planning

This set of codes was intended to distinguish between partners' use of some negotiation outside the context of actually enacting their methods of game playing from a negotiation occurring within game playing. Negotiations that occurred outside of actually enacting a game were coded as "planned" as opposed to those coded as "game-embedded" kinds of negotiations. Planned negotiations were expected to be associated with several types of interactive and game level measures of complexity.

Planned negotiations—negotiations that were not prompted by nor incurred during the act of playing the game.

Embedded negotiations—negotiations that were directly prompted by game activity (either when playing the game or when setting it up) and were initiated during game play.

III. GAME COMPLEXITY COMPONENTS

Game complexity codes reflected the evolving logical structure of the game as it was constructed by successive negotiations that continually established rules or procedures that marked changes in the overall method of playing the game. There were three sets of codes that reflected different dimensions of evolving game complexity. They were: (1) change indicators, (2) change components, and (3) backward pathway. Change components and backward pathway codes were used to maintain a running score of the emergent level of game complexity.

Change indicators

Negotiations that yielded an increase in game complexity level were distinguished from those negotiations that did not yield a change in game complexity level (i.e., No-change vs. Change-up). These codes were used to mark the effects of given negotiations on evolving levels of game complexity.

Change components

Change component codes indicated the types of rules or procedures in a negotiation that affected an increase in the level of complexity of the game construction. These codes were identified and hierarchically organized according to a priori task analyses of common board games. They reflected increasingly more complex types of rules and goals that complicated and/or constrained the methods or conditions of playing a game. If a given negotiation involved more than one change component, the higher ordered code was indicated. The nine components reflected increasing levels of game complexity. They were: (1) the first introduction of a designation or procedural rule, (2) the first conditional rule, (3) the first goal, (4) the first system of scoring, (5) the first additional goal, (6) every occurrence of a constraining rule, (7) every complex conditional rule, (8) every rule for an alternative pathway, and (9) every goal for an alternative pathway.

Backward pathway

A priori task analyses of common board games also indicated that rules that caused a reversal in the forward movement of pieces toward a goal, or the loss of pieces needed to attain a goal, marked critical changes in increasing the complexity of the game. For example, a conditional rule might specify that if a game piece lands on a particular marker, the player must move that piece to a previous place on the board that, in effect, sets that player back from where he or she was in terms of attaining a goal or subgoal. Negotiations that specified the conditions for a backward path for one or more game pieces were coded and were used as an additional indicator of the level of game complexity.

Levels of game complexity

The level of game complexity was coded as a sequence of numbers that continually reflected, at the end of any given negotiation, the current complexity level of a game in construction. Level of complexity was scored according to how the various types of rules or procedures (i.e., change components) from a negotiation affected the evolving logic of the game. Thus, for example, the first time a negotiation had the effect of introducing a rule regarding a system of scoring, the complexity of the game was increased by one level from its previous level. The game complexity level also was increased each time a negotiation effected a rule that specified a backward pathway. If a negotiation had the effect of abolishing one or more preexisting rules or goals, the level of game complexity was reduced by one level.

A complete set of operational definitions along with examples of all the codes are in the coding manual in the appendix.

INTER-CODER RELIABILITIES

Perspective coordination scores

Initial threshold reliability for perspective coordination scores from participants' responses to the 11 probes on Selman's (1980) friendship dilemma was computed by two investigators independently scoring a random selection of 20% of participants' responses ($n = 36$). Inter-rater reliability was obtained by dividing the total number of agreements by the total number of agreements plus disagreements. Initial threshold reliability was 82%. After establishing initial reliability, every fifth protocol ($n = 29$) was independently scored by two investigators. Ongoing inter-rater reliability for 20% of the sample ranged from 82% to 100% ($M = 84\%$).

Table 4
Ongoing Inter-Rater Reliabilities of Dyadic Interaction Codes

Codes	Percent Reliability		Kappa
	Range	$\underline{M}$	
Conversation turn functions	80 - 90	84	.76
Conversation turn justifications	91 - 100	97	—
Negotiation outcomes	80 - 91	85	.78
Negotiation game topics	83 - 96	90	.75
Negotiation planning	82 - 100	93	—
Game change components	80 -100	90	.80
Game backward pathways	87 - 100	97	—

Note: Those codes without kappas were dichotomous.

Interaction codes

A random sample of pilot data was used by four coders for training and then for independently establishing initial inter-rater reliabilities. When pairs of coders independently established a threshold of no less than 80% reliability for each of the interaction codes on a sample of 15 protocols and without further modifying the operational definitions of the codes, they began coding parsed transcripts from the sample protocols. Prior to coding interactions, transcripts were parsed to identify which conversational turns initiated and which resolved each negotiation. Initial reliability for parsing the transcripts was no less than 80%.

Inter-coder reliability for parsing the transcripts was computed by dividing the number of conversational turns that coders independently agreed constituted a negotiation (from initiation to resolution) by the greatest number of conversational turns that either coder coded as a negotiation. Inter-coder reliabilities for each of the interaction codes were computed by dividing the total number of agreements by the total number of agreements plus disagreements.

Once coding began, every fifth transcript was independently coded by two investigators to ensure continuity of reliability. Accordingly, ongoing inter-coder reliabilities were obtained from a random selection of 20% of the protocols ($n = 18$). Ongoing inter-coder reliability for parsing ranged from 80% to 88% ($M = 84\%$). In addition to the percent of agreement, Cohen's kappa statistic was used to measure reliability for codes in which there was less than 90% reliability in order to provide feedback to the coders for point by point disagreements. All coder differences were resolved through mutual consensus among the coders. Ongoing inter-coder reliabilities for the interaction codes are reported in Table 4.

4

Differential Analyses

We begin by reporting significant differences among the proportions of the dyadic interaction codes (i.e., kinds of conversational turns and kinds of negotiations) and whether they varied as a function of grade, gender, or game complexity. However, there were few differences in interaction codes according to either grade or gender effects. We then consider dyadic mean differences in measures of perspective coordination and create several dyadic ratio scores to reflect the mutual balance or synchronicity in partners' interactive activities. In the next chapter, we discuss the rationale for the kind of sequential analyzes that were performed and then report findings from analyses of sequential patterns of conversational turns and how they came to define the four different kinds of negotiations and how these, in turn, were associated with levels of evolving game complexity. Hence, findings from the sequential analyses reported in the next chapter build upon the findings reported in the present chapter and provide a conceptually more advanced sense of how knowledge is jointly constructed by going beyond analyses of simple proportions of interaction codes and testing their effects according to sequential patterns.

Proportions were computed for each dyad by dividing the number of targeted codes by the total number of codes within a given code set for that dyad. Thus, for example, proportions for the different kinds of negotiations were computed by dividing a given kind of negotiation by the total number of negotiations for a given dyad. Arcsin transformations were used on all of the analyses in order to correct for skewness of distributions. Unless otherwise noted, differences among the mean proportions within any given code set were analyzed by 3 (Grade) X 2 (Gender) X (set of proportions for a given code set) repeated measure AN-OVAs that included the Greenhouse-Geisser correction for departure from compound symmetry. Unless otherwise noted, there were no significant main or interaction effects involving grade or gender. Post hoc analyses were done using the Neuman-Keuls statistic at the .05 level of significance.

SIMPLE FREQUENCIES OF CONVERSATIONAL TURNS AND NEGOTIATIONS

There was a mean of 86.64 conversational turns per dyad ($SD = 51.53$; range = 16 to 232) and 5.78 mean conversational turns in a negotiation ($SD = 1.61$; range of dyadic means = 2.89 to 10.67). There was a mean of 14.92 negotiations per dyad ($SD = 7.24$; range = 2 to 41). None of these indices differed across grade or gender. Table 5 lists the means and standard deviations by grade and gender for the frequency of conversational turns per dyad, conversational turns per negotiation, and negotiations per dyad.

PROPORTIONS OF CONVERSATIONAL TURNS

Frequencies for three conversational turn codes—demonstrations, qualifications, and compromises—were not sufficient to maintain them as independent codes, so they were combined with other conceptually related codes: demonstrations with clar-

Table 5
Mean Frequencies and Standard Deviations of Conversational Turns, Turns per Negotiation Episode, and Negotiation Episodes by Grade and Gender

Grade	Boys		Girls		Total	
	M	SD	M	SD	M	SD
	Conversational Turns					
First	84.00	47.23	86.53	53.50	82.77	47.60
Third	96.60	42.99	94.07	63.68	95.33	53.40
Fifth	72.20	63.03	86.47	40.17	81.83	52.14
	Conversational Turns per Negotiation Episode					
First	5.95	1.54	5.88	1.56	5.92	1.53

Table 5 (Continued)

Third	6.31	1.42	5.78	1.69	6.04	1.56
Fifth	5.43	1.96	5.31	1.46	5.37	1.70

Negotiation Episodes

First	14.33	7.47	13.60	6.99	13.97	7.11
Third	15.73	6.28	15.33	7.53	15.67	6.82
Fifth	13.06	6.40	17.27	8.87	15.17	7.53

ifications and qualifications and compromises with elaborations. This resulted in a revised set of 10 conversational turns.

Conversational turns

There were significant differences among the proportions of conversational turns, $F(9, 756) = 178.90$, $p < .001$. The highest proportion of conversational turns consisted of elaborations ($M = .25$), followed by initial proposals ($M = .19$), followed by agreements ($M = .17$), which was followed by disagreements ($M = .09$). The proportions of ignore/asides, elicitations, clarifications, and counter proposals were not significantly different from each other (M's = .07, .06, .06, & .05, respectively) but were significantly greater than the two remaining conversational turns: confirmation requests and repetitions (Ms = .03 & .03).

Justified conversational turns

There was a significantly greater proportion of unjustified compared to justified conversational turns (Ms = 94.67 vs. 1.66, & 3.67, respectively), $F(2, 168) = 3,977.50$, $p < .001$. The proportions of perspectively and factually justified turns were combined, resulting in two categories: justified and unjustified conversational turns.

There were significant differences among proportions of different kinds of conversational turns that were justified, $F (9, 369) = 20.14$, $p < .001$. A significantly higher proportion of disagreements were justified compared to any other kinds of conversational turns. Differences among proportions of other justified conversational turns were minor since half (i.e., 54%) of all justified conversational turns were disagreements. For example, the next highest proportion was for agreements (10%). Hence, justifications were predominately associated with disagreements.

NEGOTIATIONS

The mean proportion of frequencies for four kinds of negoti-ations—ignored, withdrawn, compromise and synthesis—were too low to sustain them as independent kinds of negotiations, and, hence, they were combined with other conceptually related kinds of negotiations: ignored and withdrawn with unresolved kinds of negotiations, and compromise and synthesis with ex-pansive kinds of negotiations. This resulted in a revised set of four kinds of negotiations: unresolved, acquiescence, acceptance, and expansive.

There were significant differences among the proportions of kinds of negotiations, $F(3, 352) = 160.24.$ $p < .001$. There was a greater proportion of acceptance kinds of negotiations compared to the other three kinds, and the proportion of acquiescence kinds of negotiations was greater than unresolved and expansive kinds of negotiations ($Ms = .56$ vs. .18 vs. 15, & .11, respectively).

Length of negotiations

Kinds of negotiations differed in terms of their mean number of conversational turns (i.e., length), $F(3, 114) = 54.88, p > .001$. Expansive kinds of negotiations had a greater number of con-versational turns than the other kinds of negotiations. Unre-solved and acceptance negotiations had a greater mean number of conversational turns than acquiescence kinds of negotiations ($Ms = 10.06$ vs. 5.59 & 5.50 vs. 2.41, respectively).

Proportions of conversational turns across kinds of negotiations

The four different kinds of negotiations were distinguished according to their relative proportion of different kinds of con-versational turns. In a 3 (Grade) X 2 (Gender) X 4 (Kind of ne-gotiation) X 10 (Kind of conversational turn) ANOVA, there was a significant kind of negotiation by kind of conversational turn

interaction, F (27, 1026) = 2.65, $p < .001$. This was further analyzed in a series of 3 (Grade) X 2 (Gender) X 4 (Kind of negotiation, repeated measure) ANOVAs on the relative proportions
of each of the conversational turns. Table 6 reports significant
differences in the mean proportions (and standard deviations) of
conversational turns across the four kinds of negotiations.

Reading the columns from Table 6, we see that different negotiations were composed of different kinds of conversational
turns. Reading the rows, we see that significant differences were
obtained across negotiations for proportions of initial proposals,
counterproposals, disagreements, agreements, and elaborations.
There was a larger proportion of initial proposals in acquiescence
kinds of negotiations and a smaller proportion in expansive
kinds of negotiations. However, because there was one initial
proposal to every negotiation, this finding simply reflected the
brevity of acquiescence kinds of negotiations, on one hand, and
the length of expansive negotiations, on the other. Of more interest was a significantly smaller proportion of counterproposals
in acquiescence kinds of negotiations, a greater proportion of
disagreements in unresolved kinds of negotiations, a greater proportion of agreements in acquiescence and acceptance kinds of
negotiations, and a greater proportion of elaborations in expansive kinds of negotiations. The only gender difference was a significantly higher proportion of counterproposals among girls, F
(3, 114) = 3.51, $p < .05$ (Ms = 11.13 vs. 4.62).

How the conversational turns were differentially distributed
across the four kinds of negotiations are best explained by particular 2- and 3-chain sequences of conversational turns that
were associated with different kinds of negotiations. These sequential analyses are reported in the next chapter.

Kinds of negotiations and increases in game complexity

In this analysis, we were interested in learning whether some
kinds of negotiations were more likely than others to yield in-

Table 6
Means (and Standard Deviations) of Proportions of Conversational Turns Across Types of Negotiations

Conversational turns	Types of Negotiations				F (3, 114)	p<
	Unresolved	Acquiescence	Acceptance	Expansive		
Initial Proposal	25.03^b (12.03)	42.85^a (9.98)	20.22^b (6.12)	11.98^c (5.94)	82.5	.01
Counter Proposal	8.98^a (12.74)	1.87^b (5.45)	5.94^a (4.75)	5.87^a (5.66)	6.82	.01
Disagreement	29.41^a (20.73)	1.63^c (6.03)	7.46^b (6.42)	5.55^b (7.08)	20.61	.01
Agreement	5.34^c (9.06)	28.82^a (19.19)	19.28^b (7.70)	13.48^b (7.23)	35.27	.01
Elicitation	5.96 (9.52)	3.47 (9.15)	6.65 (4.26)	4.31 (5.65)		ns

Repetition	2.28 (4.25)	0.67 (2.62)	3.38 (4.04)	2.98 (4.55)		ns
Elaboration	14.22[c] (12.92)	5.70[d] (9.64)	19.71[b] (6.79)	42.45[a] (13.54)	78.56	01
Confirmation Request	2.31 (4.88)	1.13 (5.26)	4.10 (4.05)	2.25 (3.69)		ns
Ignore or Aside	11.20 (15.90)	11.36 (17.36)	5.82 (6.36)	5.74 (4.85)		ns
Clarification	4.27 (6.75)	1.51 (4.15)	7.43 (5.60)	5.39 (5.99)		ns

Values with different superscripts within columns differ significantly, a>b>c>d creases in levels of evolving game complexity. Twenty-two percent of all negotiations resulted in increases in levels of game complexity. In a 3 (Grade) X 2 (Gender) X 4 (The proportion of instances that each kind of negotiation increased level of game complexity) ANOVA, there was a significant main effect for the proportion of increases in game complexity among the four kinds of negotiation, F (3, 114) = 22.70, $p < .01$. Expansive kinds of negotiations were most likely to lead to increases in evolving game complexity, followed by acquiescence and agreement negotiations (Ms = .54 vs. .23 & .24). Not surprisingly, unresolved kinds of negotiations never advanced game level complexity.

Also, negotiations associated with increases in game level complexity had a significantly greater number of conversational turns compared with negotiations that were not associated with increases in game complexity, F (1, 83) = 34.37, $p < .001$ (M = 7.43 vs. 5.14).

Summary of findings regarding negotiations

Findings reported so far reflect systematic differences in the properties of different kinds of negotiations. These differences are consistent with our theoretical model of collaborative cognition which posited that the four kinds of negotiations reflect increasing levels of intersubjectivity by which the board games were jointly constructed and enacted. The different kinds of negotiations differed in terms of their length, their composition of conversational turns, and their likelihood of being associated with increasing levels of game complexity. Expansive negotiations were the longest, contained the highest proportion of elaborated conversational turns, and were most likely to result in increases in levels of game complexity. By contrast, unresolved negotiations were brief, had a high proportion of disagreements, and did not lead to any increases in levels of game complexity. Acquiescence negotiations were the briefest and primarily consisted of simply an initial proposal followed by an agreement; a quarter of them led to increases in levels of game complexity.

Acceptance negotiations were the most frequent kinds of negotiations. They also were brief but contained a variety of conversational turns: elaborations, agreements, disagreements, and counterproposals. An interesting yet unexpected finding concerned the distribution of disagreements across negotiations. Disagreements were one way by which participants might have questioned the adequacy of their partner's reasoning and, hence, they might have reflected sociocognitive kinds of conflicts that could have led to productive resolutions relative to game level complexity. Instead, however, disagreements were most likely to occur among unresolved kinds of negotiations, so that even when they were justified, they alone did not typically generate game constructions. In the next chapter, when we report findings from sequential analyses of conversational turns by kinds of negotiations, we will have a better sense of the role of disagreements as they co-occur, in sequence, with other conversational turns.

Finally, the absence of grade and gender effects on the proportion of conversational turns and negotiations is noteworthy. We will return to the issue of grade effects (or lack thereof) when we consider other developmental markers and other ways of examining cognitive change.

PLANNED AND EMBEDDED NEGOTIATIONS

There were two contexts in which negotiations could have occurred that reflected some sense of planning on the part of participants: (1) prior to partners initiating the enactment of the game that they were co-constructing and (2) when they stepped aside from their game enactment after it had been initiated. Both ways reflected a degree of preconceiving a method of game activity outside of the context of game enactments. Negotiations that occurred during participants' game enactments are considered to have occurred in the absence of planning and are referred to as embedded negotiations. Because 90% of all planned negotiations occurred at the start of interactions prior to participants initiating any kind of game enactment, we will limit our analyses of planning to this context.

Dyads had a mean of 6.02 planned negotiations (range = 2 to 28) that occurred prior to any game enactments and 40.2% of all kinds of negotiations were planned. This did not differ significantly by either grade or gender. Planned negotiations had more conversational turns than embedded negotiations, F (1, 79) = 56.94, $p < .001$ (M = 7.21 vs. 4.68).

In order to test for differences among kinds of negotiations in terms of whether they took place on- or off-task (i.e., planned or embedded), the proportion of negotiations was analyzed in a 3 (Grade) X 2 (Gender) X 4 (Relative proportion of each kind of planned negotiation, repeated measure). There was a significant main effect for the relative proportion of planned negotiations, F (3, 114) = 8.21, $p < .001$. Expansive kinds of negotiations were more likely to have occurred off-task prior to game enactments, reflecting a planning function, than unresolved and acceptance kinds of negotiations which, in turn, were more likely than acquiescence kinds of negotiations (Ms = 70.37% vs. 53.28%, 40.80% vs. 28.19%).

Another way of looking at the effect of planning was to correlate the number of planned negotiations prior to the first game-enacted negotiation with the level of game complexity achieved by a dyad at the close of their collaboration. This correlation was .25 ($p > .05$, R^2 = .06), but it was qualified by a significant quadratic trend, which was tested by a multiple regression analysis containing both linear and quadratic trend components, F (1, 87) = 6.66, $p < .01$, R^2 = .13. There was a positive relation between the number of initial planned negotiations and game level complexity, up to 11 planned negotiations (i.e., the higher the number of initial planned negotiations, the higher the level of game complexity achieved), which then became flat among dyads whose number of initial planned negotiations exceeded 11. In other words, the number of planned negotiations did not contribute to game complexity after 11 occured in a dyad.

Summary of findings regarding planned negotiations

These findings address certain issues regarding the joint planning and the joint execution of plans. All dyads went through a phase of planning their game procedures prior to attempting to test the feasibility of their ideas by actually beginning to play the game with one another. These kinds of negotiations were more actively co-constructive than those that occurred during the course of enacting the game. They had more conversational turns and a higher proportion of them were of the most developed (expansive) kind of co-construction and the lowest proportion of them were of the least developed (acquiescence) kind of co-construction. Such findings might also reflect the collaborative nature of having to co-construct a game, which involves the most basic and complex kinds of negotiations occurring first and prior to enactment, and then, once game playing begins, further negotiations could be more directed at adjusting the basic rudiments of play that already had been established. Our analyses of game topics speaks to this possibility.

Consistent with these and prior findings, the amount of planned negotiations was significantly associated with the levels of game complexity achieved, but the association stopped at 11 negotiations. It was as if those participants who exceeded 11 initial planned negotiations did not achieve high levels of game complexity because they lost sight of the purpose of their engagement—to jointly construct a game that they could actually play—and thus failed to carry out, within the threshold of 11 negotiations, the plans they had been formulating.

GAME COMPLEXITY

Evolving levels of game complexity were indicated at each negotiation according to the kinds of rules and goals that were negotiated (i.e., game topics). In this way, measures of game complexity were designed to capture the evolving changes in how a game was being jointly constructed and in what ways it was emerging as a more complex form of a rule-based board game. As described in the coding manual, negotiations involving the first introduction of the cognitively simpler rules of play (designation rules and procedural rules) and the first goal increased the evolving level of game complexity, as did the introduction of each and every more complex kind of rule, such as constraining rules and conditional rules and subsequent goals that qualified the first goal. In this way, every negotiation was coded according to whether it had the effect of either increasing or not increasing the evolving level of game complexity according to the game topic negotiated. There were no instances in which negotiations had the effect of decreasing levels of game complexity.

Our first analysis of game complexity is simply a test of grade and gender effects on the highest level of game complexity achieved. There was a main effect for grade, F (2, 84) = 4.65, p < .05. Fifth and third graders achieved significantly higher levels of game complexity than first graders (Ms = 5.1 and 4.6 vs. 3.6, respectively).

Negotiation episodes by evolving game complexity levels

The next analysis captured microgenetic changes in how a game evolved across negotiation episodes for each dyad. Figure 1 depicts the sequential mean changes in game complexity levels across negotiation episodes from one to ten. Changes in game complexity levels from the first through third turns of interaction (there was not sufficient statistical power to test at the fourth episode and beyond) were analyzed. There was a significant effect for negotiation episode and a significant grade by negotiation episode interaction, $F(2, 166)$ = 28.92, p < .01 and $F(4, 166)$ = 2.43, p = < .05, respectively. By the second and third negotiation episodes, participants in the third and fifth grades

Figure 1
Mean Game Complexity Level as a Function of Negotiation Episode by Grade

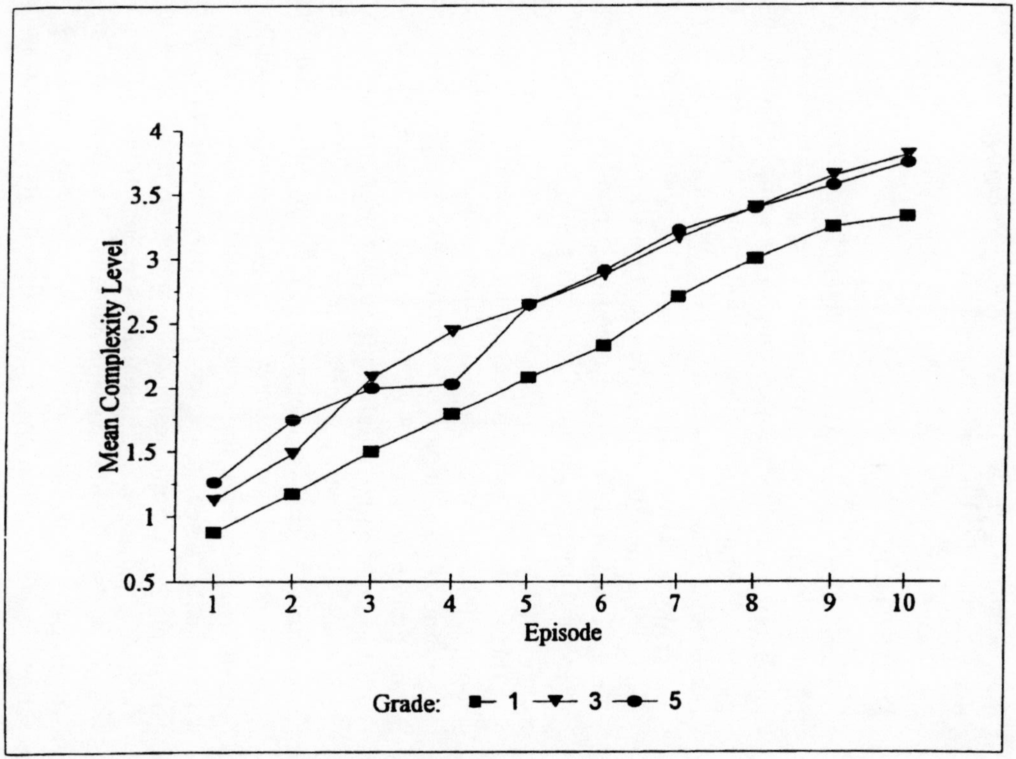

Grade: ■— 1 ▼— 3 ●— 5

achieved significantly higher levels of game complexity than did first-grade participants (M = 1.67, 1.90 vs. 1.27, respectively, at the second negotiation episode and 2.20, 2.17 vs. 1.57, respectively, at the third negotiation episode).

GAME TOPICS

The kinds of game topics negotiated by participants were defined by their rule-based functions. It was hypothesized that game topics would vary according to their implied levels of complexity, ranging from designation rules, procedural rules, conditional rules, and constraining rules. Hence, we expected associations between the complexity of game topics and (1) grade levels and (2) the complexity of the kinds of negotiations. First, we report differences in the proportions of game topics by grade and then the relation between game topics and kinds of negotiations.

There was a significant interaction between grade and game topic, F (8, 336)= 3.89, p < .001. There was a significantly higher proportion of conditional rules among fifth graders than first and third graders (Ms = 27.8 vs. 16.6 & 16.6, respectively); however, third graders had a significantly higher proportion of constraining rules than first and fifth graders (Ms = 4.8 vs. 1.7 & 1.6, respectively). This finding reversed the hypothesized place of conditional and constraining rules in the range of game topic complexity. Instead, the developmental pattern for game topic complexity, when grade level was used as an index of development, went from designation and procedural rules to constraining rules to conditional rules. Constraining rules had the same if/then form as conditional rules; however, they referred to rules that had previously been negotiated, whereas conditional rules involved an if/then rule within a given negotiation.

Game topics by kinds of negotiations

In our next analysis, we found that game topics were associated with kinds of negotiations, $F (12, 456) = 1.79, p < .05$. The highest proportion of designation rules were associated with unresolved kinds of negotiations, followed by proportions of procedural and conditional rules, and then by constraining rules and goals ($Ms = .18$ vs. .11, .11, vs. .04, .06, respectively). The highest proportion of conditional rules, constraining rules, and goals were associated with expansive kinds of negotiations, followed by designation rules and procedural rules ($Ms = .25, .20, .24,$ vs. .09, .11, respectively). The proportions of game topics in the other kinds of negotiations (i.e., acquiescence and acceptance negotiations) did not differ.

Summary of findings regarding game topics

Evolving levels of game complexity increased from first to third grade and were apparent by the third negotiation of game construction. Parallel with the increase in evolving game complexity, there was a shift toward more complex game topics, and more complex game topics were associated with more complex kinds of negotiations. The particular relationship between conditional and constraining rules and goals with expansive kinds of negotiations supports our overall premise regarding the nature of more complex kinds of negotiations allowing for the negotiation of more complex topics of game construction.

REGRESSION ANALYSIS ON LEVELS OF GAME COMPLEXITY

The level of game complexity achieved was analyzed in a multiple regression analysis with step-wise elimination of variables against all of the variables with which it was significantly correlated: (1) dyadic mean perspective coordination scores, (2) proportion of unresolved kinds of negotiations, (3) proportion of expansive kinds of negotiations, and (4) total number of negotiations. The resulting equation retained three variables and explained 40% of the variance of game complexity level, F (3, 86) = 20.69, $p < .001$. The level of game complexity achieved could be predicted by the dyads' proportion of unresolved negotiations (negative association, $r = -.32$, $p < .001$), their number of negotiations ($r = .50$, $p < .001$), and their proportion of expansive kinds of negotiations ($r = .22$, $p < .01$; partial correlation coefficients).

PERSPECTIVE COORDINATION

As a dyadic index of the cognitive maturity of partners collaborating in a dyad, the mean of each of their mean perspective coordination scores was computed. Correlations were then computed between their dyadic mean perspective coordination scores and their dyadic interaction codes, including (1) number of conversational turns, (2) proportion of conversational turns, (3) number of negotiations, (4) proportion of kinds of negotiations, (5) length of negotiations, and (6) game complexity levels. The dyadic mean perspective coordination scores were positively correlated with the number of conversational turns ($r = .23$, $p < .05$), number of negotiations ($r = .29$, $p < .01$), and game complexity level, ($r = .35$, $p < .01$). Among the different kinds of conversational turns, the dyadic mean perspective coordination scores were negatively correlated with the proportion of elaborations ($r = -.22$, $p < .05$) but were positively correlated with the proportion of confirmation requests ($r = .22$, $p < .05$) and justifications ($r = .29$, $p < .01$). Among the different kinds of negotiations, the dyadic mean perspective coordination scores were negatively correlated with the proportion of unresolved negotiation outcomes ($r = -.21$, $p < .05$).

Regression analysis with age as a covariate

Because perspective coordination scores were associated with grade level (F [1,174] = 8.55, $p < .01$ [Ms = 1.15 vs. 0.91 vs.

0.56, for fifth, third, and first grades]), age was entered as a co-variate in a multiple regression on dyadic mean perspective co-ordination scores with step-wise elimination of variables. The interaction variables that were correlated with the dyadic mean perspective coordination scores also were entered into the re-gression equation: (2) number of conversational turns, (3) num-ber of negotiations, and (4) game complexity level. The resulting equation retained two of the four variables (game complexity level and proportion of elaborated conversational turns) and ex-plained 45.8% of the variance of the dyadic perspective coordi-nation scores, $F (3, 86) = 26.05, p < .001$. The standardized partial regression coefficients were age as covariate ($r = .57, p < .001$), game complexity level ($r = .20, p < .05$), and proportion of elab-orations ($r = -.19, p < .05$). Thus, independent of age, the dyadic mean of participants' ability to coordinate perspectives was pos-itively associated with the level of game complexity they achieved but negatively associated with their proportion of elab-orated conversational turns.

That participants' ability to coordinate perspectives was neg-atively associated with their proportion of elaborated conversa-tional turns might seem to challenge the theoretical significance of perspective coordination in the co-construction of knowledge. However, it was less important that mean perspective coordi-nation scores were negatively correlated with elaborated conversational turns than the finding that they were positively correlated with levels of game complexity because game com-plexity was a more direct measure of the benefits of collaborative cognition than the proportion of elaborated conversational turns. Although findings so far might seem to challenge the microge-netic thrust of elaborated conversational turns in how they allow for one partner to build on the thinking of the other in discourse that proceeds from one conversational turn to the next, as will be shown in the next section of the present chapter and in the next chapter, this occurs only when elaborated conversational turns are computed as a simple proportion of conversational turns in a negotiation. In the next section, we report that the mutual synchrony, or balance, between partners' use of elaborated kinds of conversational turns has important consequences. Also, in the next chapter, when reporting findings from a series of sequential analyses, we find that when elaborated conversational turns were analyzed according to their place in a sequence of conversational turns constituting a negotiation, they were associated with a variety of negotiations that promoted collaborative cognition.

DYADIC SYNCHRONY BETWEEN PARTNERS

Because dyadic activity was the basic unit of analysis, it was important to study the effects of the extent of symmetrical or asymmetrical sharing between partners in putting forth proposals for constructing their games. In other words, did it matter among dyads whether one partner tended to dominate the other in certain aspects of negotiating or whether both partners shared more equally in the interaction? In order to index the extent of balance or synchrony between partners' relative contributions when interacting, findings from ratio scores are reported for two kinds of conversational turn codes: elaborations and initial proposals (ratio scores from the other conversational turn codes did not yield theoretically relevant findings). Ratios were computed by taking the smaller score of interest for a partner in a given dyad and dividing it by his or her partner's larger score. Ratios, therefore, ranged from zero to one; the higher the ratio score, the greater the balance or equality of dyadic activity between partners.

Ratio of proportion of elaborated conversational turns

The ratio of elaboration kinds of conversational turns was important because of its implications for providing a means for one partner to discursively act on the thoughts of the other partner and also because of the previously reported finding of a negative association between the proportion of elaborated kinds of conversational turns and the dyadic mean perspective coordination scores. The ratio of the proportion of elaborations was correlated with (1) the ratio of the proportion of initial proposals ($r = .26$, $p < .01$); (2) the ratio of the proportion of agreements ($r = .28$, $p < .01$); (3) the number of conversational turns ($r = .31$, $p < .01$); (4) negatively correlated with the proportion of acceptance kinds of negotiations ($r = -.22$, $p < .05$); and (5) positively correlated with the proportion of expansive kinds of negotiations, ($r = .21$, $p < .05$). These findings suggest that, when partners in a dyad are more likely to each act off of the ideas of one another in a balanced fashion so that each has a shared role in elaborating upon the proposals of the other, they will be more likely to initiate negotiations (e.g., by offering initial proposals) for the other's consideration. Furthermore, a greater synchrony between partners in their use of elaborations yielded a greater number of conversational turns, which resulted in a greater proportion of developmentally more complex kinds of negotiations (i.e., expansive instead of acceptance kinds of negotiations). The above pattern of relations between the synchronicity of interactions between partners and the complexity of negotiating is further examined in the next section having to do with the sequence of conversational turns.

Regression analysis on ratio of proportion of initial proposals

We were particularly interested in the balance between partners according to their use of initial proposals because, in effect, the initial proposal not only marked the initiation of a negotiation, it defined the topic of a negotiation and influenced the next step in how a game was being constructed. In this regard, how did dyads in which each partner was as likely as the other to initiate proposals for negotiation back and forth during the discourse differ from dyads in which one partner tended to prevail over the other in terms of initiating negotiations? In order to test this, a multiple regression with step-wise elimination of variables was performed on the ratio of initial proposals as the dependent variable and the variables with which it had significant simple correlations as independent variables: (1) number of negotiations ($r = .26$, $p < .01$); (2) ratio of disagreements ($r = -21$, $p < .05$); and (3) ratio of elaborations ($r = .26$, $p < .05$). The resulting equation retained all three of the variables and explained 14% (adjusted) of the variance, $F (3, 86) = 6.01$, $p < .001$. The greater the ratio or balance between the proportion of initial proposals expressed by partners in a dyad, the lower their ratio of disagreements (i.e., the greater the disparity between partners in the proportion of disagreements expressed, $r = -.27$, $p < .01$), the greater their ratio of elaborations ($r = .22$, $p < .05$), and the greater the number of negotiations generated in discourse ($r = .23$, $p < .05$, partial correlation coefficients).

5

Sequential Analyses

INTRODUCTION

When observing and coding temporally ordered events, lag sequential analyses can be conducted to test whether there are systemic relations between prior and subsequent events. Such analyses are quite different from those that might be had by computing simple aggregates that yield mean frequencies or proportions of frequencies of coded events (such as those reported in the previous section). The sequential analysis of interaction codes allows for the determination of whether the occurrence of one event in an interaction is more likely than chance to follow or precede another event. It also allows one to determine sequential relations between events, controlling for specific variables such as gender or age across variables that cannot be had through simple correlational analyses. For example, in a simple analysis, one might find that event A is significantly more likely than chance to result in outcome X, whereas event B is not. However, in a sequential analysis, one might find that event B results in outcome X when it occurs following event C. Furthermore, it can be determined whether this sequence holds across conditions, such as older and younger participants or males and females. This capacity to statistically capture serial pattens of interacting among two or more participants advances studies of the effects of social interaction by more fully capturing the ecological and situated features of a stream of discourse and provides a statistical-descriptive approach to the analysis of social behavioral sequences (Bakeman & Brownlee, 1980; Dorval & Eckerman, 1984; Gottman, 1979; Lichtenberg & Heck, 1986). Because conversational turn interactions are, by nature, temporally sequenced and reciprocally influenced, they are particularly appropriate for sequential analyses. They permit investigators to answer questions about naturally occurring patterns of interacting between one partner and the other and about how such patterns of interacting are associated with different kinds of factors or outcomes (Bakeman & Quera, 1995a).

A particular kind of sequential analysis known as lag sequential analysis begins with the assumption of dyadic interaction as a discrete stochastic process made up of a sequence of discrete events, with each event coded in terms of a finite number of mutually exclusive and exhaustive categories. A "lag" is a term used in sequential analyses to indicate the serial position between events of interest. The first event of interest is indexed as zero (lag 0). The subsequent event is indexed as lag 1 and the event after that as lag 2, etc. According to Bakeman, Adamson, and Strisik (1989), "If we think of later events (or intervals) as lagging earlier events and if we say that the earlier event (often called the given or antecedent event) occupies lag position 0 and later events (often called target or consequent events) occupy lag positions 1, 2, etc., then the general question becomes, does behavior at lag position 0 affect behavior at lag 1? at lag 2? at lag 8? etc." (p. 245). For example, consider the following hypothetical sequence of four events: W, X, Y, Z. There is a lag 1 relation between events W and X, a lag 1 between events X and Y, and a lag 1 between events Y and Z. There is a lag 2 relation between events W and Y, and between events X and Z. There is a lag 3 relation between events W and Z.

Using log-linear methods, investigators are able to answer questions about which sequential patterns of discourse (i.e., conversational turns of talk) are associated with different kinds of outcomes. In this section, we consider the differential effects of two- and three-turn sequences of conversational turns in terms of different kinds of negotiations. In order to assess which lag 1 conversational turn sequences occurred more frequently than chance, we computed adjusted residuals based on the kind of t tests proposed by Gottman (1979) and others. The adjusted residuals compared the conditional probabilities with the unconditional probabilities (by taking the conditional probability minus the unconditional probability and dividing by an estimate of the standard deviation of the difference). Such adjusted residuals determined whether the proportion of instances of an event A following an event B was greater than (or less than) would be expected by chance. Because we were interested in how conversational turn sequences were used to progressively construct interpersonal negotiations, we focused only on instances greater than (not less than) chance. Significant adjusted residuals are considered only in cases where both the target and the given conversational turns had frequencies of at least 20 occurrences, which commonly is recommended as a minimum frequency to obtain reliable proportions (e.g., Bakeman & Gottman, 1986). Assuming comparable degrees of freedom (i.e., 30), adjusted residuals across all of the analyses exceeding 3.20 were significant at the .001 level; those exceeding 2.33, at the .01 level; and those exceeding 1.65, at the .05 level. A bonferroni correction was used to control for Type 1 errors when computing multiple post hoc tests on a single data set.

LAG 1 CONVERSATIONAL TURN SEQUENCES BY KINDS OF NEGOTIATIONS

A log-linear analysis was used to examine the relative distribution across kinds of negotiations of conversational turns that immediately followed the conversational turn, *initial proposal*. We focused on sequences of conversational turns following initial proposals because initial proposals initiated a negotiation. Because negotiations typically were brief, we expected the response to the initial proposal to set the pattern that would differentiate one kind of negotiation from another kind. Specifically, from the proportion of conversational turns that occurred across kinds of negotiations (see Table 6), we expected that disagreements in response to initial proposals would disproportionately lead to unresolved kinds of negotiations, that agreements would lead to acquiescence kinds of negotiations, that elaborations would lead to expansive kinds of negotiations, and that inquiries (i.e., the merger of elicitation, repetition, confirmation requests, and clarification conversational turns) would lead to acceptance kinds of negotiations. Counterproposals in response to initial proposals would lead to all kinds of negotiations, except acquiescence.

Preliminary analyses indicated that certain categories of conversational turns were not frequent enough to analyze alone, although they occurred in similar patterns across kinds of negotiations when they followed an initial proposal. These conversational turns were elicitations, repetitions, clarification requests, and confirmations, and, therefore, they were collapsed into a new category of conversation turns called inquiry. Thus, the 10 kinds of conversational turns that could follow initial proposals were reduced to 6: counterproposals, disagreements, agreements, elaborations, ignore/asides, and inquiries.

The design of the log-linear analysis was 3 (Grade) X 2 (Gender) X 4 (Negotiation) X 6 (Sequence). All possible effects beginning with a four-way interaction and extending down to the "base model" were determined; the base model was "Grade X Gender X Sequence on Negotiation." This meant that all interaction effects involving kinds of negotiations were assessed, but not those involving any of the other three variables. This was the appropriate base model when negotiation served as the dependent variable and the other three factors as independent variables (Bakeman & Robinson, 1994). The magnitude of each effect was assessed with Q-square, which, according to Bakeman and Robinson (1994), is comparable to R-square in regression analyses. Also, according to Bakeman and Robinson (1994), only effects with a Q-square greater than .10 are worth interpreting. In the three analyses, only the sequence by negotiation interaction had a Q-square greater than .10 (Q-square = .74). There were no grade or gender effects in these analyses. Table 7 reports frequencies, conditional probabilities and adjusted residuals pertaining to the sequence by negotiation interaction.

Bakeman and Robinson (1994) suggest that all significant residuals in a table such as Table 7 have descriptive relevance. In the present case, they indicate that different conversational turns following initial proposals were associated with different kinds of negotiations. However, these kinds of residual findings are not independent of one another (Bakeman, Robinson, & Quera, 1996), and, therefore, it is necessary to further analyze them post hoc to determine which minimum selected set of significant residuals were responsible for the overall χ^2 being significant. According to Bakeman et al. (1996), the selection of which residuals to test as a set should be made, when possible, on conceptual grounds and, in the present study, significant positive residuals were chosen to constitute the first set, followed by a second set, if statistically justified, consisting of negative significant residuals. Since we were interested primarily in how negotiations were progressively constructed, turn by conversational turn, we felt that the positive residuals, as a set, were more meaningful than the negative ones because they indicated the turns most likely to constitute the building blocks of the different kinds of negotiations. Also, if it were statistically justified to interpret all of the positive residuals, it would support the rationale for analyzing the third conversational turns in the constructive process.

Bakeman et al. (1996) prescribe an iterative post hoc procedure. In the first iteration, the residual, among those selected, having the highest value is deleted and replaced with a structural zero. Then, the overall χ^2 is recomputed. If it is not significant, the procedure is halted, and only the first residual is determined to have been necessary to account for the significant

Table 7
Results from the Negotiation X Sequence Interaction from the Lag 1 Log Linear Analysis of Grade X Gender X Sequence X Negotiation Strategy

Initial Proposal Followed by:		Types of Negotiation Strategies				
		Unresolved	Acquiescence	Acceptance	Expansive	
Counter proposal	Frequency	19	6	107	27	
	Cond. prob.	0.12	0.03	0.14	0.13	
	Adj. residual	0.08	-4.51***	2.96**	0.44	
Disagreement	Frequency	61	4	103	12	
	Cond. prob.	0.39	0.02	0.14	0.06	
	Adj. residual	9.92***	-5.45***	0.25	-3.61***	
Agreement	Frequency	13	159	152	30	
	Cond. prob.	0.08	0.75	0.20	0.14	
	Adj. residual	-5.52***	17.26***	-5.96***	-4.41***	

Elaboration	Frequency	23	4	173	94
	Cond. prob.	0.15	0.02	0.23	0.45
	Adj. residual	-2.38**	-7.80***	0.97	8.64***
Inquiry	Frequency	23	11	160	30
	Cond. prob.	0.15	0.05	0.22	0.14
	Adj. residual	-0.76	-5.00***	4.99***	-1.08
Ignore	Frequency	16	28	48	15
	Cond. prob.	0.10	0.13	0.06	0.07
	Adj. residual	1.07	2.96**	-2.51**	-0.52

*$p < .05$
**$p < .01$
***$p < .001$

χ^2. However, if the χ^2 remains significant, the residual, among those selected, that has the next highest value is deleted and replaced with a structural zero and the overall χ^2 is again computed. If this χ^2 is not significant, the procedure is halted, and the first and second residuals are determined to have been necessary to account for the significant χ^2. However, if the χ^2 remains significant, the procedure is again repeated using the residual, among those selected, that has the third highest value, and so forth until the overall χ^2 is no longer significant. In the present post hoc analysis, the overall χ^2 remained significant when each of the significant positive residuals were deleted (χ^2 = 19.0, df = 9, p < .05) and accounted for 96% of the variance (i.e., Q^2) of the two-way interaction. The overall χ^2 was then nonsignificant when the negative residual having the highest value was deleted in the iteration. It was therefore concluded that all of the six significant positive residuals (and the highest value negative residual) contributed to the significance of the overall χ^2.

Initial proposals followed by agreements (n = 354) were significantly more likely than chance to have resulted in acquiescence kinds of negotiations, a finding that makes intuitive sense. Acquiescence negotiations were quite brief (M = 2.41 conversational turns), and initial proposals followed by agreements often constituted completed negotiations. That initial proposals followed by ignores/asides (n = 107) also resulted in acquiescence kinds of negotiations was less obvious, but might have reflected a participant's implicit agreement with his or her partner's initial proposal. Initial proposals followed by counterproposals (n = 159) were significantly associated with acceptance kinds of negotiations. This kind of negotiation implied a participant's active consideration of his or her partner's initial proposal (i.e., beyond simple acquiescence), and the expression of a counterproposal established conditions for active consideration of both the initial proposal and the counterproposal. Another kind of active consideration of an initial proposal would be to question some aspect of it and, accordingly, initial proposals followed by

inquiries ($n = 224$) also were associated with acceptance kinds of negotiations. That **initial proposals followed by disagreements** ($n = 180$) led to unresolved kinds of negotiations suggested that a participant's immediate disagreement with his or her partner's initial proposal reflected a refusal to negotiate. However, as will be shown, the outcome of this kind of conversational turn sequence was qualified by how Partner A responded to B's disagreement with his or her initial proposal. Finally, **initial proposals followed by elaborations** ($n = 294$) were associated with expansive kinds of negotiations. An elaborated conversational turn constituted an expansion of the conditions proposed in an initial proposal and, thereby, established the parameters for participants to actively collaborate in the co-construction of some aspect of the game. Expansive kinds of negotiations reflected the partners' joint agreement of proposals that incorporated conditions contributed by both of them.

Together, these initial proposal lag 1 findings indicated that participants' ways of responding to their partners' initial proposals strongly influenced the outcome of the negotiations (i.e., the variance among the four kinds of negotiations was significantly associated with participants' immediate response to their partners' expression of an initial proposal).

THIRD TURN LAG 1 CONVERSATIONAL TURN SEQUENCES BY KINDS OF NEGOTIATIONS

In order to capture the kinds of responses that one partner made in reaction to his or her partner's initial proposal, we examined lag 1 conversational turn sequences. Then, in order to capture the kinds of reactions that the partner who had offered the initial proposal made in reply to his or her partner's reaction to his or her own initial proposal, we examined the sequential occurrence following each kind of two-turn sequence, that is, the third conversational turn. For expository purposes, when discussing the second and third conversational turns that followed initial proposals, we refer to the participant in a dyad making an initial proposal as Partner A and the responding participant, as Partner B. However, within any given dyad, the same participant did not consistently serve the role of Partner A and of Partner B across different negotiations. That is, whoever started a new topic was always designated as Partner A for the new negotiation.

This set of analyses was a refinement of how the negotiations were jointly constructed by extending the sequential analyses to the third turn. Because grade and gender were not significant effects in the prior log-linear analysis, they were not included as variables in these sequential analyses. The third turns that came after initial proposals followed by each of the six conversational turns from Table 7 were examined in six separate 7 (Sequence) × 4 (Negotiation) log-linear analyses. There were seven possible conversational turns that could occur as the third turn, the six in Table 7 plus the default category, "No third turn." If there were less than 10 instances of a particular two-turn chain in a given kind of negotiation, then that negotiation was ignored (Bakeman & Quera, 1995b). For example, because only six initial proposals followed by counterproposal chains occurred in acquiescence kinds of negotiations, the analysis of third turns following the sequence initial proposals and then counterproposals did not include acquiescence negotiations (i.e., a 7 × 3 instead of a 7 × 4 log-linear analysis).

There were significant sequence-by-negotiation interaction effects in each of the six log-linear analyses, and each had a Q-square value greater than .10. Therefore, post hoc analyses for determining which cells in a matrix were appropriate to interpret were done using step-wise chi-square analyses of the cell frequencies in the Sequence X Negotiation matrices. If the overall chi-square was significant (and it was in each analysis), the frequencies in cells with significant adjusted residuals were then deleted one by one in descending order according to the magnitude of a given cell's frequency. Chi-square analyses were then sequentially recomputed until at least 90% of the variance of the two-way interaction was accounted for. Those adjusted residuals representing the cells that were removed were interpreted. This was a more conservative and data-driven method of statistical analysis than that used for findings reported in Table 7 because these were exploratory analyses. The conditional probabilities, positive adjusted residuals, and alpha levels for the significant interaction effects from each of the six log-linear analyses of third-turn sequences by kinds of negotiations satisfied by this post hoc procedure are reported in Table 8.

Initial proposal followed by counterproposal conversational turn sequences

Acquiescence negotiations were not included in this log-linear analysis because of the low frequency ($n = 6$) of this two-turn chain in acquiescence kinds of negotiations. There were three significant post hoc interaction effects, $\chi^2 (12) = 3.17$, $p < .01$, indicating that the third turn in an initial proposal plus counterproposal sequence of conversational turns was differentially associated across kinds of negotiations (see Table 8). Initial proposals followed by counterproposals that were, in turn, followed by **disagreements** ($n = 27$) were more likely than chance to have resulted in unresolved kinds of negotiations. A disagreement in this sequence reflected Partner A's rejection of B's attempt to offer an alternative proposal for achieving the same ends. It is as if Partner A intended to say, "It's my proposal or nothing, and I won't consider any alternative." This, understandably, had the effect of discouraging opportunities for further construction of a mutually acceptable proposal.

When **agreements** followed as the third turn in initial-proposal-plus counterproposal sequences of conversational turns ($n = 37$), the outcome of the negotiation was most likely to be acceptance of the proposal. In many respects, this sequence is the converse of the previous three-turn sequence. Partner B's counterproposal constitutes a kind of constructive or generative disagreement, which leaves open the opportunity for Partner A to consider B's proposed expansion of Partner A's proposal.

Table 8
Significant Findings from Log-Linear Analyses of Third Turn Lag 1 Sequences in Chains of Conversational
Turns Beginning with Initial Proposals by Types of Negotiation Strategies

Initial proposal followed by

Second turn	Third turn	Type of negotiation	Conditional probability	Adj. residuals	p <
Counter proposal	Disagreement	Unresolved	0.37	2.22	.01
	Agreement	Accepted	0.29	2.47	.01
	Elaboration	Expansive	0.52	3.60	.01
Disagreement	None	Unresolved	0.31	4.43	.01
Agreement	Disagreement	Unresolved	0.15	4.95	.001
	Inquiry	Accepted	0.20	4.57	.001
	Inquiry	Expansive	0.23	2.24	.01

	Elaboration	Unresolved	0.69	2.99	.01
	Elaboration	Accepted	0.42	3.83	.01
	Elaboration	Expansive	0.70	4.75	.001
	Counter prop.	Accepted	0.05	2.15	.05
	None	Acquiesce	0.85	12.12	.001
Inquiry	Agreement	Accepted	0.17	2.05	.05
	None	Acquiescence	0.05	5.75	.001
Elaboration	Counter Prop.	Unresolved	0.21	2.01	.05
	Disagreement	Unresolved	0.29	3.79	.001
	Agreement	Accepted	0.23	1.80	.05

Table 8 (Continued)

	Elaborated	Expansive	0.49	5.52	.001
	Inquiry	Accepted	0.14	2.01	.05
	None	Accepted	0.20	3.07	.01
Ignore	Inquiry	Accepted	0.23	2.72	.01
	Elaboration	Accepted	0.52	2.64	.01
	None	Unresolved	0.63	3.21	.01
	None	Acquiesce	0.64	4.79	.001

When partner A accepts it, it is likely to result in an accepted kind of negotiation in which there has been active consideration of the proposal.

When **elaborated** conversational turns followed as the third turn in initial proposal-plus-counter proposal sequences of conversational turns ($n = 39$), there was a significant probability that the negotiation would be of an expansive kind. Elaborated conversational turns also were significantly associated with expansive kinds of negotiations when they were the second conversational turn to follow an initial proposal. In this case, Partner A moved from his own proposal to not only accepting B's counterproposal, but to explicitly expanding upon it. This mode of negotiating is associated with the most complex kind of constructive negotiation.

Comparing findings of the statistical likelihood of kinds of negotiation outcomes when two-turn sequences in which initial proposals were followed by counterproposals with three-turn sequences in which a third turn was included in the analysis, we find that two-turn cases associated with acceptance kinds of negotiations were qualified by the consideration of a third turn. Acceptance kinds of negotiations were associated with the two-turn sequences of initial proposals followed by counterproposals, but this outcome was maintained only in those cases when these conversational turns were followed by agreements. Disagreements led to unresolved kinds of negotiations, and elaborations led to expansive kinds of negotiations. Thus, when Partner B offered an alternative to his or her partner's initial proposal, conditions were set for co-constructive engagement, but only if Partner A demonstrated a willingness to consider his or her partner's counterproposal.

Initial proposal followed by disagreement conversational turn sequences

Acquiescence negotiations were not included in this log-linear analysis because of the low frequency ($n = 4$) of this kind of two-turn chain in this kind of negotiation. There was only one significant post hoc interaction effect, χ^2 (12) = 29.0, $p < .01$ (see Table 8). Initial proposals followed by disagreements followed by **no third turns** ($n = 26$) were significantly associated with unresolved kinds of negotiations. Thus, if Partner B disagreed with Partner A's proposal, and if Partner A then failed to acknowledge his or her partner's disagreement and instead changed the topic of discourse, the negotiation remained unresolved.

Initial proposal followed by agreement conversational turn sequences

There were eight significant post hoc interaction effects, χ^2 (18) = 210.4, $p < .001$ (see Table 8). **Counterproposals**, as the third turn in this particular two-turn sequence ($n = 9$), were associated with acceptance kinds of negotiations. These were cases in which, after Partner B agreed with Partner A's proposal, Partner A offered a counterproposal to his or her own proposal. This reflected a participant's further engagement with his or her own ways of constructing the game once he or she had the tacit agreement of his or her partner. This sequence of conversational turns gave evidence of having involved some level of co-constructive discourse because the outcome was likely to be an acceptance kind of negotiation rather than mere acquiescence. **Disagreements** ($n = 4$), as the third turn, were associated with unresolved kinds of negotiations. This was an infrequent kind of interaction in which Partner A, after receiving agreement with his or her own proposal, then disagreed with it. **Inquiries** ($n = 39$), as the third turn, were associated with both acceptance and expansive kinds of negotiations. In these cases, Partner A posed some sort of inquiry (or repetition) regarding conditions of Partner B having accepted Partner A's proposal. It was a generative form of interpersonal engagement leading to higher kinds of negotiations. **Elaborations** ($n = 111$), as the third turn, were associated with unresolved, acceptance, and expansive kinds of negotiations. This was a relatively common pattern of discourse after Partner B had agreed with Partner A's proposal. In these cases, Partner A extended the conditions of his or her own proposal after receiving tacit agreement from Partner B. It was as if he or she were constructing the proposal in stages, and the intention was, "OK, now that you accepted my proposal, consider this additional piece to it." Occasionally ($n = 9$), this interactive pattern was risky in that it resulted in unresolved kinds of negotiations. Yet, more often, like inquiry as the third turn, it was associated with co-constructed kinds of negotiations. Extending the sequential analyses to a fourth turn (had there been sufficient frequencies), might have differentiated between unresolved, accepted, and expansive kinds of negotiations in the initial proposal, agreement, and elaboration conversational turn sequence as well as between accepted and expansive kinds of negotiations in the initial proposal, agreement, and inquiry conversational turn sequence. Finally, when there was **no third turn** ($n = 174$) to the initial proposal—agreement conversational turn sequence—the kind of negotiation was acquiescence. This case is, almost by definition, what an acquiescence kind of negotiation is all about. Partner B simply agreed with Partner A's proposal, and Partner A moved onto another topic without prompting Partner B to further consider his or her proposal.

Initial proposal followed by inquiry conversational turn sequences

There were two significant post hoc interaction effects, χ^2 (18) = 35.5, $p < .01$ (see Table 8). **Agreements,** as the third turn in this particular two-turn conversational chain ($n = 31$), were associated with acceptance kinds of negotiations. In such cases Partner A confirmed B's inquiry about A's proposal. The confirmation maintained the interaction that led to the acceptance of the proposal. Also, when **no third turns** ($n = 13$) followed the initial proposal—inquiry sequence—negotiations ended in simple acquiescence. Partner A's failure to verbally respond to B's inquiry about his or her proposal can be seen in such cases as a tacit agreement, which perhaps might have been conveyed by gesture. This pattern was a less active level of interpersonal engagement than was the prior case of explicitly acknowledging a partner's inquiries about the initial proposal, and, thus, it resulted in acquiescence, instead of acceptance, kinds of negotiations.

Initial proposal followed by elaboration conversational turn sequences

Acquiescence negotiations were not included in this log-linear analysis because of the low frequency ($n = 4$) of this type of two-turn chain in this kind of negotiation. There were six significant post hoc interaction effects, $\chi^2 (12) = 57.1$, $p < .05$ (see Table 8). **Counterproposals** as the third turn in this particular two-turn conversational chain ($n = 26$) were associated with unresolved kinds of negotiations, **disagreements** with unresolved negotiations ($n = 26$), **agreements** with acceptance negotiations ($n = 58$), **inquiries** with acceptance negotiations ($n = 25$), **elaborations** with expansive negotiations ($n = 92$), and **no third turns** with acceptance negotiations ($n = 40$). Taken together, these findings indicated that how Partner A responded to B's elaboration upon A's proposal differentiated among the four kinds of negotiations. These findings speak to the fecundity of how a participant chooses to deal with his or her partner's attempts to expand upon or contribute to his or her proposal, and they go to the heart of the co-constructive nature of interpersonal negotiations. Although unresolved negotiations were not frequent in this sequence pattern, they occurred when Partner A either disagreed with or made a counterproposal in response to B's attempt to elaborate on A's proposal. It reflected A's unwillingness to consider his or her partner's engagement. In order for a negotiation to end in an agreement, Partner A needed to implicitly (no third turn) or explicitly agree to B's elaboration or inquire about it so as to acknowledge and maintain the interaction.

When Partner A elaborated upon B's elaboration of Partner A's proposal, the pattern was set for the negotiation to be expansive and thus reflected the mutual contributions of each participant in formulating a proposal.

Initial proposal followed by ignore/aside conversational turn sequences

There were four significant post hoc interaction effects, χ^2 (18) = 67.2, $p < .001$ (see Table 8). Both **inquiries** and **elaborations** as the third turn in this particular two-turn conversational chain (ns = 14 & 41, respectively) were associated with acceptance kinds of negotiations. These third turns reflected Partner A's successful attempt to keep the interaction moving along despite Partner B having failed to acknowledge Partner A's proposal. In one case, Partner A explicitly questioned Partner B about the proposal and, in the other, Partner A, despite Partner B's having ignored the proposal, elaborated upon his or her own proposal, which presumably had the effect of reengaging Partner B in the co-construction, resulting in a negotiation in which the proposal was accepted by both of them. When there were **no third turns** (n = 31) to the initial proposal—ignore/aside sequence of conversational turns—negotiations either were unresolved or acquiesced, reflecting either a failure to co-construct a proposal or to unilaterally accept Partner A's proposal.

SUMMARY OF FINDINGS FOR THE SEQUENTIAL ANALYSES

Table 9 summarizes the log-linear analyses of second- and third-turn sequences of chains of conversational turns in negotiations, beginning with initial proposals and arranged according to serial patterns of conversational turns associated with each of the four kinds of negotiations.

Unresolved and accepted kinds of negotiations consisted of a larger array of significant conversational turn sequences than ac-

Table 9
Significant Second and Third Turn Conversational Sequences Following Initial Proposals by Types of Negotiations

Type of negotiation	Initial proposal	+	Second turn	+	Third turn
Unresolved			counter prop.	+	disagreement
			disagreement	+	none
			agreement	+	disagreement
			agreement	+	elaboration
			inquiry	+	disagreement
			elaboration	+	counter prop.
			elaboration	+	disagreement
			ignore	+	none

Acquiescence

| agreement | + | none |
| ignore | + | none |

Accepted

counter prop.	+	agreement
agreement	+	inquiry
agreement	+	elaboration
agreement	+	counter proposal
inquiry	+	agreement
elaboration	+	agreement
elaboration	+	inquiry
elaboration	+	none
ignore	+	inquiry

97

Table 9 (*Continued*)

	ignore	+	elaboration
Expansive			
	counter prop.	+	elaboration
	agreement	+	inquiry
	agreement	+	elaboration
	elaboration	+	elaboration

quiescence and expansive kinds of negotiations, but for different reasons. From Table 9, it can be seen that there were many different patterns of discourse that led participants either to fail to resolve their negotiations and put forth a proposal (unresolved kinds of negotiation strategies) or to actively engage one another and accept an initial proposal (accepted kinds of negotiations). In contrast, negotiations in which a participant simply acquiesced to his or her partner's proposal consisted of only two patterns of conversational turn sequences (agreement or ignore following an initial proposal). The finding that the agreement-plus-elaboration sequence of conversational turns occurred in unresolved, accepted, and expansive kinds of negotiations suggests that, among three turns of discourse, elaborations alone did not distinguish among these three kinds of negotiations. What matters, then, is how a participant responded to his partner's elaborated conversational turn in the fourth turn. However, in the second and third turns among three turns of discourse, a participant responded to his partner's elaborated conversational turn with another elaborated conversational turn only in expansive kinds of negotiations.

On the basis of several criteria, expansive kinds of negotiations were found to be the most complex kind: (1) Conceptually, they involved the contributions of both participants in negotiating and accepting a proposal that went beyond the confines of the initial proposal and incorporated conditions contributed by both participants. (2) They had a greater number of conversational turns and a greater proportion of elaborated conversational turns (the ratio of which was positively correlated with the proportion of expansive negotiations). (3) A greater proportion of these kinds of negotiations were planned compared with other kinds. (4) They were more productive than other kinds in terms of the proportions of conditional rules, constraining rules, and goals with which they were associated. (5) They were associated with a higher proportion of increases in the game level complexity achieved than each of the other kinds of negotiations. Despite the complexity of expansive kinds of negotiations, or, perhaps

Table 10
Illustrated Patterns of Sequences of Conversational Turns Associated with Expansive Types of Negotiations

Participant A: First turn	Participant B: Second turn	Participant A: Third turn
Initial proposal: *Hey, I know, let's use the spinner to see who goes first.*	Agreement: *Yea that's great. I wanna do that.*	Inquiry: *OK, but then what color goes first?*
Initial proposal: *Hey, I know, let's use the spinner to see who goes first.*	Agreement: *Yea that's great. I wanna do that.*	Elaboration: *Yea, and whoever gets on the blue goes first*
Initial proposal: *Hey, I know, let's use the spinner to see who goes first.*	Elaboration: *Yea, and whoever gets on the blue goes first*	Elaboration: *Yea, and you gotta put your piece on the first blue on the board*
Initial proposal: *Hey, I know, let's use the spinner to see who goes first.*	Counter proposal: *No, let's use the dice, it's better.*	Elaboration: *Yea, and the highest number goes first.*

because of it, they were defined by only four patterns of conversational turn sequences, three of which included elaborated conversational turns and the fourth, an inquiry which served as a kind of request by a participant making an initial proposal for an elaboration of his or her partner's agreement with the initial proposal. Thus, the present findings operationally defined the process by which one partner, elaborating upon ideas expressed by the other, attained a developmentally advanced, (i.e., expansive) mode of interpersonal engagement.

As a means of illustrating the ways by which dyadic partners reciprocally operate on each other's reasoning according to the discourse features of a expansive kind of negotiation, we offer, in Table 10, examples of a given initial proposal followed by four patterns of second- and third-turn conversational sequences that were statistically associated with expansive kinds of negotiations (i.e., an agreement followed by an inquiry, an agreement followed by an elaboration, an elaboration followed by an elaboration, and a counterproposal followed by an elaboration).

6

Discussion

In discussing the present findings, certain differences need to be considered in the conceptualization, design, and methodological analyses that distinguish the present study from prior studies of children's collaborative cognition. The purpose of the present study, unlike many previous studies in this field of inquiry, was neither to train children to acquire particular interaction strategies nor to test how particular interaction strategies advance their solitary cognitive reflections. Instead, we chose to systematically capture the sequential flow of children's dyadic interaction as it related to their co-construction of knowledge and ways of knowing.

Hence, the design of the present study differed from more traditional studies along several critical dimensions that led, in turn, to some new ways of conceptualizing children's peer collaborations. Most notably, we adopted a sociocultural approach, in which our unit of analysis was the collaborative activities of the dyad instead of the residue or "outcome" of such activities in terms of participants' individual competencies. According to Rogoff (1998), a sociocultural approach constitutes a paradig-

matic shift from examining the "social influence" of one child's
activities upon another child's to examining cognitive development as a collaborative process by which modes of interpersonal
engagement are "constituted by and themselves constitute cultural practices" (p. 722). It is in the transactions between people
where culture is created. By contrast, a "social influence approach" treats the individual as the unit of analysis and consid-
ers social interaction as an influence on individual development.
It recognizes the social and culturally mediated features of
knowing in terms of relatively inert functions having to do with
some form of internalization. This, in turn, raises vexing questions regarding the nature of cognitive mechanisms that could
account for the internalization of knowing and allow for quali-
tative advances in individual cognitive competencies (see Furth,
1968; Lawrence & Valsiner, 1993; Wertsch, 1993; Arievitch & van
der Veer, 1995 for contributions to the "internalization debate").
A sociocultural approach, by explicitly acknowledging a method
of active co-construction, circumvents the internalization conun-
drum because it posits knowledge as being collaboratively constructed through cultural forms of interpersonal activities that
involve discourse, cultural artifacts and cognitive tools that are
expressed in the context of their modes of engagement (Stetsenko
& Arievitch, 1997).

Opportunities for participants in the present study to construct
board games collaboratively created a social context that yielded
ways of studying their cognitive development consistent with
the core assumption of a sociocultural approach. Instead of using
hypothetical logical-reasoning kinds of problems with a finite set
of solutions and then measuring the effects of interaction by
comparing pre- to postinteraction changes in individual competencies (a social influence approach), the collaborative process,
in the present study, was relatively informal and open-ended. It
engendered a type of knowing that was immediate and situated
in terms of its deployment in activities that were highly familiar
among children of the ages sampled.

AGE EFFECTS

A basic question one might ask regarding the present findings is how they changed as a function of participants' ages, which ranged from 6 through 10 years. Age was not associated with the mean length of negotiations (number of conversational turns per negotiation), the mean number of negotiations, or the different proportions among kinds of negotiations. Neither did the proportion of planned negotiations nor the proportion of negotiations that were justified vary as a function of age. Also, age did not enter into significant associations between kinds of negotiations by conversational turns.

There were, however, significant age effects for measures that marked the cognitive complexity of the games that participants were co-constructing. Hence, fifth graders had a significantly higher proportion of negotiations about conditional rules than first and third graders, and third graders, a higher proportion of negotiations about constraining rules than either first or fifth graders. Negotiations about conditional and constraining rules were associated with the evolution of more complex kinds of games, so that age effects in collaborative development were seen in the levels of game complexity achieved. In this regard, we can conclude that it wasn't how participants negotiated, but what it was they negotiated about, that affected the game complexity levels they achieved. Games constructed by fifth and third graders were more complex than those constructed by first graders, and the complexity of their constructions was evident by their second and third negotiation episodes.

If we consider game complexity as our measure of achievement and ways of interacting (e.g., length, number, or kinds of negotiation episodes by conversational turns) as our measure of process, the present findings are reminiscent of Werner's (1937) classic distinction between process and achievement in development and reflect how similar processes can lead to different levels of cognitive developmental achievement. In the present case, we see how means of negotiating ways of co-constructing games that are independent of age yield evolving game structures that cognitively vary as a function of age.

Participants' capacity to coordinate self/other perspectives, another kind of process variable, was a more compelling developmental marker of the quality of interpersonal engagement than was their age. In order to maintain the integrity of the dyadic unit of analysis, we used participants' dyadic mean scores on Selman's (1980) measure of levels of perspective coordination. We found that, even when factoring out age as a covariate, a significant degree of variance in game complexity levels was accounted for by participants' dyadic mean perspective coordination scores. The association between the dyadic mean perspective coordination scores and game complexity levels suggests that co-constructing complex games depends, to a significant extent, on how well participants are able to coordinate each others' perspectives.

So, we find that although different ways of interacting were not associated with age, they were associated with levels of game complexity. Therefore, one needs to look beyond age in order to account for developmental changes—changes having to do with mediating links between conversational turns, kinds of negotiations, and evolving levels of game complexity based upon the coordination of self/other perspectives.

NEGOTIATING AND PLANNING

Opportunities for participants to negotiate methods and procedures of play without actually engaging in game playing provided a means of studying the role of planning as an innovative way of looking at a metacognitive skill in collaboratively constructing knowledge. Although early studies of planning implied that children were not successful planners before their transition to formal operations, more recent studies have found that even preschoolers are quite capable planners providing the activities used to measure their planning behavior are simplified by (1) externalizing the representation of the goal state, (2) reducing the number of elements involved, and (3) placing activities in a familiar story frame, such as planning activities adapted from children's common experiences with grocery shopping or attending birthday parties (Friedman & Scholnick, 1997). Activities that involve shared task responsibilities are likely to enhance young children's propensity to plan. Activities in the present study involved shared turn-taking opportunities that made the planning process particularly explicit because, in order to proceed with enacting a mutually competitive board game, participants were obligated to negotiate common, yet rudimentary, rules of play either before or during their joint engagement in the activity (Gauvain & Rogoff, 1989; Goodnow, 1997; Hartup, 1985). What was notable, however, is that participants typically planned how to construct the game prior to playing it.

Present findings confirmed that, at each grade sampled, children planned their activities prior to enacting them. Forty percent of negotiations were planned kinds of negotiations, and 90% of them occurred prior to any attempts to execute game proposals. Also, there were several indicators that this kind of preconceiving game activities contributed to the logical complexity of the co-constructed games. Planned negotiations had a higher number of conversational turns than embedded negotiations, and 70% of planned negotiations were expansive kinds compared to only 28% that were acquiescence kinds of negotiations. In addition, the number of planned negotiations (i.e., negotiations occurring prior to the first embedded negotiation), up to 11, was significantly associated with levels of achieved game complexity. These findings confirm the facilitating effects that joint collaborations have on children's planning, particularly when collaborations occur in highly motivating, familiar, shared, and practical contexts.

KINDS OF NEGOTIATIONS

The basic units among the interactive variables in the present study were the conversational turns that were generated back and forth between participants collaborating in a dyad. Statistically, they were shown to progressively define the cognitive consequences of different kinds of negotiations. Different kinds of conversational turns were associated with different kinds of negotiations, which, in turn, were associated with different levels of evolving game complexity. This occurred both as a function of the distribution of the proportion of different kinds of conversational turns and as a function of the sequential patterns among both two- and three-turn sequences of conversational turns. Together, findings defined distinguishing features of intersubjectivity among the four kinds of negotiations. They varied in terms of levels of interpersonal complexity that ranged from (1) unresolved kinds of negotiations, in which there was no construction; to (2) acquiescence kinds of negotiations, in which the construction reflected the contribution of a single participant; to (3) acceptance kinds of negotiations, in which the contribution of one participant was acknowledged and actively considered by the other; and to (4) expansive kinds of negotiations, in which a successfully negotiated proposal reflected the active and transformative contributions of both participants. In these ways, each kind of negotiation reflected a progressively more co-constructive mode of interpersonal engagement. Negotiations differed not only in their length (i.e., mean number of conversational turns) but, more significantly, in their sequential patterns of conversational turns.

When we considered how different kinds of negotiations advanced the logical complexity of the co-constructed board games, we found that, according to several criteria, the more co-constructive components of negotiating were associated with increasing levels of game complexity as they evolved negotiation by negotiation. Expansive negotiations, in this regard, were the most developed kind because they (1) were more likely to have occurred during planning phases of game co-constructions, (2) had a greater mean length of conversational turns, (3) had a greater proportion of elaborated conversational turns, (4) were associated with the dyadic balance between partners' expressions of elaborated conversational turns (i.e., when partners expressed more equal proportions of elaborated conversational turns, they constructed a greater proportion of expansive kinds of negotiations), (5) were associated with a greater proportion of conditional and constraining rules and goals, and, (6) subsequently, were more likely than any of the other kinds of negotiations to result in methods of constructing games that advanced the level of game complexity.

CONFLICTS AND DISAGREEMENTS

An abiding interest among developmentalists (e.g., Schafer, 1968; Valsiner & Cairns, 1992) is the theoretical role that conflicts are assumed to play among most theories of development. Nowhere is this more evident then in cognitive developmental theories, particularly Piaget's, in which sociocognitive kinds of conflicts are hypothesized to induce interpersonal disequilibrations that have the potential to advance cognitive development (Piaget, 1934, 1967, 1995; see also Bearison, 1991; Chapman & McBride, 1992; Shantz & Hartup, 1992). This idea of sociocognitive conflicts leads us to privilege the expression of disagreements between participants as a kind of engagement that warrants special attention. Disagreements frequently have been used in interaction studies to index the expressive component of sociocognitive conflicts that constitute a necessary, if not sufficient, cause for disequilibrations that advance cognitive development. According to Hartup (1992), "Most investigators use disagreement frequencies, as these occur in the interaction between individuals, as criterion measures [of conflict]" (p. 188). However, previous findings from studies of children's peer interaction have been equivocal about the facilitating or the cognitively generative role of disagreements in collaborative discourse. For example, among those who measured the direct expression of the proportion of disagreements during children's discourse, Berkowitz and Gibbs (1983) and Damon and Killen (1982) found an inverse relation between the expression of disagreements and evidence of positive changes on individual pre- to posttest measures (see also Martin, 1985; Tudge, 1985). This led them to conclude that partners who accepted and transformed, but did not explicitly disagree with, each other's ideas showed the greatest cognitive gains.

Findings that generally support the cognitive value of disagreements in dyadic discourse have been reported by Ames and Murray (1982), Emler and Valiant (1982), Light and Glachan (1985), Maitland and Goldman (1974), Miller and Brownell (1975), and Walker (1983). These investigators concluded that disagreements in peer discourse have the potential to generate sociocognitive kinds of conflicts along with the accompanying need to consensually resolve them. This, in turn, is thought to motivate participants to consider the other's perspective on the common inquiry and, hence, to shift the focus from their own reasoning to accommodate reasoning about the other's expressed ideas in order to coordinate them relative to the perspectives of both the self and other. In this regard, although all disagreements need not reflect the generation or resolution of sociocognitive conflicts that advance cognitive discourse, their presence, along with the felt need to resolve them is considered to be a necessary but not sufficient condition to account for the developmental benefits of collaborative cognition. The role of disagreement in sociocognitive conflicts that are thought to advance modes of reasoning has been a continuing source of confusion, particularly with regard to increasing interest in the cooperative contexts in which advanced levels of argumentation occur (Dorval & Gundy, 1990). It calls for a different way of conceptualizing and measuring disagreements in discourse, one that more fully recognizes disagreements in the context of higher level purposes of achieving mutual agreement.

In the present study, disagreements, when scored simply as a relative proportion of the overall distribution of kinds of conversational turns, were not associated with productive kinds of negotiations. The greatest proportion of them were associated with unresolved kinds of negotiations and, contrary to previous findings (e.g., Bearison, Magzamen, & Filardo, 1986), it did not matter whether or not they were justified (although most justifications occurred in the course of disagreement kinds of conversational turns).

When the effects of disagreements were evaluated using sequential analyses, there was an association between disagreements and unresolved kinds of negotiations. This occurred when disagreements occurred as either a second or third turn in a sequence of conversational turns following an initial proposal. Second-turn disagreements reflected Partner B's disconfirming A's initial proposal. Third-turn disagreements reflected Partner A's disconfirming B's reaction to A's initial proposal. Furthermore, disagreements were the only conversational turn positively associated with unresolved kinds of negotiations when they were a reaction, in the second turn of a conversational sequence, to an initial proposal. They also were associated with unresolved kinds of negotiations when they were Partner A's reaction, in the third turn, to B's counterproposal, agreement, or elaboration.

From these findings, we conclude that, although sociocognitive conflicts might promote cognitive growth, it is not clear that such conflicts are occasioned or represented by the direct expression of such types of cognitive disconfirmations as those that we and others typically have coded as partners explicitly disagreeing (justified or not) with one another. Questions follow, then, about whether the direct expression of disagreements has the desired effect of promoting a need or a sense to consensually resolve disputes by negotiation between participants or whether these disagreements have the effect of disengaging participants from a disposition to negotiate further. Thus, we were led to consider other ways of conceptualizing how disagreeing in collaborative discourse can promote ways of knowing.

Damon (1994) also questioned the value of the direct expression of disagreements in joint activities and concluded that "some tasks encourage certain forms of interaction, but other tasks encourage other forms. Noting which tasks go with which forms is a crucial step toward understanding the developmental links between social and cognitive processes" (pp. 141–142). The present study involved a task that, compared to the more formal, often hypothetical, types of problem-solving situations occasioned in most studies of children's collaborative cognition, was more fluid, in that it was guided by emergent goals (rather than goals solely predetermined by an investigator), it was activity based, and it allowed a greater range of interpersonal agility occasioned by the absence of a finite solution or outcome. It is possible that, because problem-specific types of interpersonal engagements are more dependent on participants' willingness to directly consider certain aspects of task-related information, they might be more associated with the expression of interpersonal disagreements about processing this kind of information. In the kind of interactions occasioned by the context in the present study, however, disagreements between participants were less productive than other discursive means of negotiating.

If disagreements are not a compelling force that moves discourse in a constructive (i.e., developmental) direction, then what are some of the defining characteristics of constructive kinds of negotiations? We might also question how other kinds of conversational turns, such as counter proposals, clarifications, elicitations, and some kinds of elaborations provide a less direct means of argumentation but contribute to augmenting and transforming the other's way of thinking without directly disagreeing with it. Whether we choose to mark constructive kinds of negotiations according to the topic of discourse (the rules that prescribe the procedures of playing the game being constructed), the likelihood of any given negotiation advancing the evolving complexity of game co-constructions, or the final level of achieved game complexity, present findings indicated that constructive kinds of negotiations had features that mutually extended, refined, completed, and reflected one participant's reasoning in regard to the other. These ways by which participants cognitively operated on and transformed each other's ideas can be considered a kind of "interactive logic" (Berkowitz & Gibbs, 1983; Broughton, 1982; Piaget, 1995). This kind of reasoning upon the reasoning of another was reflected in what we coded as expansive kinds of negotiations. In comparison to the three other kinds of negotiations—unresolved, acquiescence, and accepted—expansive negotiations were the beginning of the defining parameters of interactive logic in discourse. In this kind of negotiated discourse, one participant added conditions to the other's proposal without violating its integrity, as tested by the other's willingness to concede to the added conditions. Accordingly, dyads who co-constructed the most complex kinds of board games had a higher proportion of expansive compared to any other kinds of negotiations (and, in turn, had a lower proportion of unresolved kinds of negotiations). Also, a greater proportion of expansive kinds of negotiations occurred during the initial planning phase of game co-construction compared to any of the other kinds of negotiations.

In terms of the contents of negotiations (the formal features of what the negotiations were about), the highest proportion of conditional rules, constraining rules, and goals occurred in expansive kinds of negotiations. Although it is intuitively clear how games with a greater number of goals (and subgoals) might be more hierarchically complex, the complexity of a game also was advanced by relations among its different types of rules. Both conditional and constraining rules represented more developed and complex forms of game procedures than designation or procedural rules. Conditional rules built upon procedural rules but specified an if/then kind of proposition. Constraining rules imposed limits or boundaries upon previously negotiated procedures. Thus, it made sense that negotiations about these procedures of play would be the topics of expansive kinds of negotiations and would be associated with more complex levels of achieved game complexity. These rules constituted a kind of

transformative logic that was not present in designation or procedural rules.

When achieved levels of game complexity were taken as an
indicator of the cognitive productivity of collaborative interactions, 40% of its variance was explained by three variables. The
first variable was the number of negotiations in the interaction,
the second, the proportion of negotiations that were expansive,
and the third, which was a significant negative predictor of game
complexity, was the proportion of unresolved kinds of negotiations. Thus, we can conclude from these findings that the key to
achieving high levels of co-constructive mastery in collaborative
cognition is to generate a relatively high proportion of expansive
kinds of negotiations and to avoid too high a proportion of unresolved kinds of negotiations. The latter are associated with
disagreements about what can be negotiated, and this leads participants to disengage from the negotiating process.

Elaborated conversational turns

If the turn-by-turn interactions in expansive kinds of negotiations were not marked by the occurrence of disagreements, then
what was it that set them apart from the other kinds of negotiations? Expansive kinds of negotiations had a high proportion
of elaborated kinds of conversational turns, turns by which participants augmented the conditions of their partners' game proposals. Expansive negotiations had almost half of all of the
elaborated turns (but less than 6% of all of the disagreements).
Elaborated turns were the only second-turn sequence following
initial proposals that were associated with expansive kinds of
negotiations. Thus, one defining characteristic of an expansive
negotiation is having a participant augment the other's initial
proposal rather than simply disagreeing or agreeing with the
proposal (the latter, leading to a simple agreement kind of negotiation). Findings from the third-turn sequence allowed us to
further define the properties of cognitively constructive kinds of
discourse. Three out of the four third-turn sequences associated

with expansive kinds of negotiations had elaborated conversational turns. They included Partner A elaborating upon B's (1) counterproposal, (2) agreement, or (3) elaboration of A's initial proposal. The fourth option, Partner A inquiring about B's agreement with A's initial proposal, also advanced the negotiation beyond simple acceptance to an expansive kind of negotiation.

Given this association between elaborated kinds of conversational turns and expansive kinds of negotiations, it is notable that Dorval and Eckerman (1984) also found that elaborations were kinds of conversational turns that were associated with developmentally advanced means of co-constructing topics of discourse among peers in dyads. However, they found that elaborated turns occurred primarily among participants older than those in the present study. We suspect that this was because they studied free discourse without any constraints about partners actually having to engage one another in turn-taking, rule-based, competitive game playing. These kinds of constraints have the effect of advancing development toward cognitively more co-constructive levels of interpersonal engagement than does free discourse (Stetsenko & Arievitch, 1997).

Beyond expansive kinds of negotiations

When we initially considered developmental features of interpersonal negotiations, we included two kinds of negotiations with features that exceeded those of expansive kinds of negotiations. They were what we called *compromise* and *synthesis* kinds of negotiations. Whereas, in an expansive kind of negotiation, a participant transforms a proposal by adding to the conditions of the other's proposal, in compromise and synthesis kinds of negotiations, a participant operates on the reasoning of another to somehow more clearly and radically transform the proposal. How the proposal was transformed was considered a developmental marker of the complexity of the negotiation. Hence, in compromise kinds of negotiations, participants materially incorporated the conflicting claims or reasons of their dispute after having established their mutual conflicts, and, in synthesis kinds of negotiations, they integrated aspects of each other's conflicting claims such that the mutually agreed-upon proposal was a dialectic synthesis of the thesis and antithesis kind rather than a material compromise of conflicting claims. However, we found that participants in the present study did not generate either compromise or synthesis kinds of negotiations. In this sense, they confirmed Berkowitz and Gibbs' (1983) contention (consistent with findings from Gibbs, Schnell, Berkowitz & Goldstein, 1983), that such types of higher order levels of "transactive reasoning" require formal operational modes of thinking. Hartup et al. (1993), using a social interactive context similar to the present one (i.e., having participants negotiate resolutions about divergent rules in a board game that they were playing), also found little evidence of compromise as a mode of resolving differences among 9- and 10-year-old participants.

7

Constructive Features of Collaborative Cognition

When interest in children's collaborative cognition moved beyond the pretest/interaction episode/posttest paradigm, cognitive developmental psychologists began opening the "black box" to directly observe some of the discursive features of children's ways of interacting with one another in problem-solving contexts. At the same time, sociolinguists and cultural anthropologists also began to emphasize interactive processes by which skilled and differentiated patterns of communicating and interacting emerge (e.g., Brenneis, 1988; van Dijk, 1985). Following Piaget's ideas about the value of egalitarian discourse and sociocognitive conflicts (Chapman & McBride, 1992), some cognitive developmentalists turned to the study of interpersonal conflicts in problem solving situations. However, it soon became apparent that the expression of sociocognitive conflicts was not always made manifest simply by the expression of task-relevant disagreements. More often than not, the disconfirmation of another's ideas in adversarial negotiated discourse was so reciprocally intertwined that its communicative expression and interpersonal function were obscured by conventional methods of coding discourse that relied on aggregated proportion of use scores. Speech, along with accompanying gestures and kinesics is, in this regard, an interactive activity that is continuously subject to reinterpretations as it evolves. Such reinterpretations are embedded at different levels of organization, as one conversational turn follows another. For example, a clarification or an inquiry might be embedded in an explanation, that, in turn, might be embedded in a disagreement (Garvey & Shantz, 1992). Thus, the embededness and structural complexity of all discourse, but particularly discourse constrained by interpersonal activities in sociocultural contexts that, inevitably must be negotiated, makes it unlikely that sociocognitive types of conflicts are captured by explicit expressions of disagreement with the expressed perspectives of another participant. Moreover, not explicitly disagreeing with one's partner does not necessarily reflect a participant's failure to recognize the need to coordinate his or her own perspective with another's. We conclude from the present findings that there is something more going on here.

According to theories of argumentation (argumentation being a particular form of adversarial discourse that captures the logical transformative nature of how we interact), negotiations are kinds of arguments having qualities that set them apart from mere quarrels, expressions of disagreement, or conflicting judgments (Miller, 1987). According to Chapman and McBride (1992), "To the extent that persons engage in [negotiated kinds of] argumentation, they do not merely express their disagreements, but also cooperate in discussing them" (p. 63). Findings from the present study demonstrate how this occurs in a relatively spontaneous and practical collaborative context.

Similarly, we recognize that such metacognitive skills as planning, monitoring, and evaluating are reciprocal responsibilities that are shared intersubjectively between participants such that relations between cognitive operations and communicative competencies in collaborative activities enable and give form, each to the other. However, we further note that such metacognitive skills are more likely to be displayed when participants engage in relatively unstructured and spontaneous task situations. Hence, the idea of peer conflicts, as derived from Piaget's social equilibratory model of cognitive development, and the idea of intersubjectivity and interpersonal cooperation, as derived from Vygotsky's culturally mediated model of cognitive development, are quite compatible and theoretically complement each other when considered in the context of practical activities such as the one we observed (Bearison, 1991; Cole & Wertsch, 1996; Kitchener, 1996; Rogoff, 1990). Their compatibility lies in the recognition between participants of the need not to simply disagree with one another but to engage together in the felt need to agree to cognitively struggle to clarify, augment, and elaborate upon each other's ideas. This can then become the basis for amplifying their negotiated discourse.

It is clear to us from present findings that children's cognitive development is supported by mutually reciprocal activities among peers, guided by conditions of intersubjectivity that enable them to transform one another's ideas (Cole & Wertsch, 1996). Such types of activities are the principal source of children's cultural assimilation (Harris, 1995). Therefore, how these kinds of interpersonal activities develop remains an important question for further research. From present findings, we suspect that it has to do with the means by which children acknowledge the cognitive contributions of others and yet are able to go beyond this by cognitively transforming, augmenting, and elaborating upon the other's cognitive contributions. Children's cognitive development has to do with ways by which they are able to interact with their peers that lead them to recognize and value the need to coordinate differences between the perspectives of self and others because of the mutual benefits that inhere within. According to Tomasello (1998), this "serves to motivate them toward certain goals, to instruct them in the pursuit of those goals, and, in general, to potentiate cognitive skills that would not develop in social isolation. . . . [they] make human cognition social and cultural, indeed collective, in a very fundamental way" (p. 222). This position regarding the development of children's collaborative cognition is congruous with the central role that Vygotsky (1962) accords to culturally mediated discourse in the development of thought, and the role that Piaget accords to the kind of egalitarian discourse that typically occurs among peers, involving the joint coordination of cognitive operations.

CONCLUSION

The essential problem of development in collaborative cognition is how new patterns of activity develop from the resolution of existing ones among individuals interacting in sociocultural contexts. How new patterns emerge inevitably involves some process of negotiation leading to resolutions that can be ordered along a continuum of developmental change, ranging from less to more complex emergent patterns. Such a view of the development of collaborative cognition assumes a type of epigenesis consistent with core assumptions of theories about self-regulating systems (Thelen & Smith, 1998; Oyama, 1985). However, because these self-regulating cognitive activities are socially distributed among peers, they are further understood according to specific developmental mechanisms proposed by Piaget (1950, 1967, 1995) and Vygotsky (1962, 1978).

We found that coding turn-by-turn conversations among peers jointly participating in the co-construction of enactable board games enabled us to define sequential patterns of discourse that represented a continuum of developmental change from less to more complex kinds of collaborative cognition. We examined such change, not only in terms of the ways by which children negotiate with each other, which constitutes the developmental core of interactive discourse, but also in terms of the logical complexity of the pattern of rules that emerged from their negotiated discourse and that microgenetically came to comprise the game that they were collaboratively constructing.

We believe that the present methods of coding negotiated peer interaction can be extended chronologically to study ways by which adolescents and adults interact with one another. The present methods also lend themselves to sociocultural contexts beyond those captured by rule-governed board games. The key, however, is to provide a means by which participants feel mutually engaged and spontaneously motivated to interact with one another in activities that promote shared and negotiated discourse. Such methods are likely to reveal ways by which participants build upon and advance each others' knowledge and ways of thinking.

Commentary

Sociocultural Activity as a Unit of Analysis: How Vygotsky and Piaget Converge in Empirical Research on Collaborative Cognition

Anna Stetsenko

Psychology today is gradually coming to grips with what is a trivial yet paramount idea long known to laypersons—the idea that human beings are profoundly social and collaborative by nature. People rarely act alone, and even when they appear to be doing just that, it typically is only at the surface of the process. Consider, for example, a writer who creates a novel in the solitary confinement of her house. The writer is alone only in a very narrow sense, indeed, she is writing, typically, about people, with people, and for people. The process of writing a novel can hardly be reduced to an individual cognitive reflection. Thus, the imaginary reader is always present in the creative process of writing—as an addressee, a possible judge of the creation, and, more generally, a partner in a dialogue that each human creation ultimately is. Our writer arguably also is motivated by specifically human, social purposes, such as to be understood, respected and needed by others. Perhaps even more importantly, the novelist is using a vast amount of both material and symbolic artifacts that alone make the whole process of creation possible; she is using language to express her thoughts and ideas and the certain rules of a literary style to make her creation intelligible, along with concrete products such as paper, computer, or a simple pen to materialize her thoughts. All of these have been created and produced by countless other people—contemporaries as well as members of past generations of human civilization.

Indeed, in each and every human activity, people employ, and often also develop, the fruits of human civilization—the mediational means that have been derived from cultural, historical, and institutional forces and that are embodied in language, patterns of behavior, social conventions, art, and other specifically human ways of doing, perceiving, understanding, and expressing ideas. People who produce and use these mediational means to interact with one another and achieve various goals create a specifically human sociocultural dimension of the world into which children are born and which they come to join as competent participants. Children learn from other members of their community and also from the experiences of previous generations how to act in specifically human ways—for example, how to regulate their own behavior, to take into account interests of others while setting and pursuing their own goals, to become aware of their social standing and role, and, consequently, to ground their behavior in prescribed pragmatic conventions and rules. In general, their life from birth to death is profoundly enmeshed in the complex fabric of human society and other people's lives.

This example is provided here to illustrate the point that a human being—including one's mental apparatus, the mind—is part of a wider, specifically human, sociocultural system entailing other people, rules, and conventions of social life, as well as artifacts that embody and make possible the transition and utilization of specifically human experiences of living and acting in the world. Accordingly, cognitive development can only be understood as a collective process determined by the sociocultural system to which it belongs and as immersed in all of a person's activities embedded in the local settings and cultures in which these activities are carried out.

The theoretical work of the Russian psychologist Lev S. Vygotsky was an important catalyst in bringing this critical idea to the fore of American psychology in the last decade. However, psychology has experienced, and continues to experience, difficulties in translating such general sociocultural tenets into specific research strategies and methodologies. Too often, sociocultural claims serve simply as an attractive ornament that decorates research conducted according to traditional prescriptions of the old individually oriented cognitivist science. For example, although an increasingly widespread recognition of the social and collaborative nature of human development typifies much of today's psychology, various authors interpret it in drastically divergent ways and, in many cases, individual minds continue to be the sole focus of investigation.

Consider the following specifications provided in an article by Nickerson written for a book on distributed cognition (Salomon, 1993). According to Nickerson, cognition is distributed and social in the sense that "the same people act differently in different situations, that people are influenced by the social and cultural contexts in which they live, that what one can do depends to a large degree on the tools and materials at one's disposal, that there are countless useful tools in the world including many that simplify cognitive tasks, that what skills people develop depend in part on the kinds of artifacts they must use, that it is easier to do certain things in some environments that in others, that two heads are (sometimes) better than one, that specialization of function within groups is often useful, that it is a waste of time and effort to keep some types of information in one's head" (Nickerson, 1993, p. 231). In our view, the central meaning of what is social about the mind cannot be reduced to this collection of statements. The problem is not that the complex and serious issues are expressed in a rather banal form (that was an intent of the author), but that the most serious implications of what it means to assert that cognition is social and distributed is completely missing from this description.

The reason for that is that many of the general metatheoretical claims about the collaborative nature of cognition and human development are not "taken down the road" of deriving specific implications from them by those who adhere to the tenets of sociocultural approach. This, perhaps, is the underlying reason for some authors to state that bringing Vygotskian theory into contemporary discourse has been a complicated venture and that his works are still not well understood, especially in North America (e.g., Tudge & Scrimsher, in press). Deriving implications from metatheoretical claims is not a minor task because, as is the case with all broad overarching ideas, "the devil hides in the implications," and only by exposing these implications can one get to see the real meaning and import of the initial general assumptions.

Only in recent years have efforts been undertaken to convert the long established lip-service paid to Vygotsky and other sociocultural psychologists into concrete approaches and research methodologies (cf. Gellatly, Rogers, & Sloboda, 1989). Bearison and Dorval provide a wonderful illustration of this progress. Their research is remarkable in several ways. First and foremost, it shows how to move beyond merely declaring the importance of human interaction for developmental research to actually studying the developing mind in ways that are truly congruent with the idea that humans are social and collaborative by nature. As a result, Bearison and Dorval's research helps to elucidate a set of interrelated implications from the sociocultural theory with a clarity—too often missing in this field—as to how these implications necessarily change our research strategies of defining, conceptualizing, and studying developmental processes.

The first profound implication is that the development of individuals cannot be understood and studied in isolation from the interpersonal relations in which they are immersed. This also means that the unit of analysis in psychological research is not the individual mind but the social context of interpersonal activity. As Bearison and Dorval maintain, taking this idea seriously means that it is not just a matter of attending to how children interact and then proceeding to test the effects of such interactions on each individual child's cognitive functioning. In other words, it is not a matter of simply taking into account some sociocultural influences on individual development in an additive fashion, as an additional variable that also impacts the individual mind. Instead, if we indeed understand the development of cognition as a collaborative process, our unit of analysis—that is, what the researcher looks at, measures, and analyzes—has to be the social engagement itself, engagement that captures the social, cultural, and historical functions of conjoint activity within a problem solving system.

Both theoretical and empirical efforts in Bearison and Dorval accordingly are focused on analyzing this social engagement in its various forms, in contrast to research paradigms that single out one child for analysis and, thereby, preclude opportunities to observe the very process by which children acquire knowledge. The words "the very process" are a key to understanding the dialectics between the individual and collective mind and a safeguard against a simplified view of their relationship. Certainly, intraindividual cognitive functions can be abstracted from the reality of collective sociocultural activities at a certain, and usually rather mature, stage in the development of each of these functions. In that sense, Bearison and Dorval are correct to mention that the "sociocultural mind" is as much a reflection of the "individual mind" as is its converse (p. 12). However, I believe that this statement of a dialectical interdependence should not conceal the central idea of the sociocultural theory (especially elaborated by Vygotsky's follwers in the so-called activity theory framework, see, e.g., Gal'perin, 1989; Leont'ev, 1978) that studying intraindividual cognition offers a culturally constrained method of capturing only the end-product of what, from a genetical viewpoint, is necessarily a collective interindividual process. In other words, the individual mind is certainly real, but, from a sociocultural perspective, the individual mind is always only a relatively independent individual enactment of processes previously formed in collective cultural practices. Accordingly, in order to understand how children's minds develop and how individuals acquire new knowledge, one has to go beyond individual cognition and study interindividual collective engagements.

The second related implication of the sociocultural perspective that Bearison and Dorval advance is that the human mind is experientially located not in the head of an individual and not in some abstract space between people, but "out there" in the reality of what children actually do while collaborating, that is, in the very fabric of their collective activities. This seemingly simple change in the mind's "location" signifies a radical shift from the assumption that the human mind must be described in terms of symbols, images, ideas, and other forms of mental representations—an assumption typical of cognitivist research orientation that dominated psychology over the last several decades. The metaphor of mind as located "not in the head" means that, instead of a shadow process hidden in the depths of a mental machinery of each individual child, or some purely semiotic dynamic of mysterious collective representations, the sociocultural collaborative activities that children participate in need to be the main focus of investigation in developmental research.

This assumption does not carry with it implications of sociocentrism or semiotic reductionism (Bearison & Dorval, p. 3). Again, the focus is on what children do, without assuming that performance is simply a clouded window of competence. Accordingly, this shifts the focus from achievement (outcome) to process (engagement), in congruence with Werner's legacy. This also is congruent with the central Piagetian claim that mental constructs derive from children's active elaboration of general coordinations of actions and thus are themselves a form of activity rather than a mysterious superstructure "in the head." Finally, this position is a concretization of the Vygotskian claim that social relations among people genetically underlie all higher psychological functions. Bearison and Dorval are right to give credit, especially, to these two giants of developmental psychology—Vygotsky and Piaget—throughout their efforts.

It is important to emphasize that this position means that cognition is taken to be not a mysterious capacity detached from real-life processes, but exactly as a see-it and hear-it process that takes place "right before our eyes" in the activity of social exchange between people. Moreover, this activity always emerges first as a practical activity in the material world and only subsequently, through complex transformations, does it become more detached (although never completely isolated) from material collective processes. In other words, all processes of the human mind must be material and collective before they become subjective, psychological, and individuated.

The third and related implication that Bearison and Dorval advance is that the cultural mediation of social interaction is central to studying the developing mind. An individual's activities are interwoven with conventions and artifacts that constitute an essential part of a concrete relation between humans and their sociocultural environment. This implies that cultural tools are not merely additional variables that somehow affect the mind in a rather extraneous fashion, for example, by reducing the amount of mental effort that people have to expend to accomplish specific goals. On the contrary, cultural tools should be viewed as essential parts of the very process of human mentation and subjectivity.

This view of cultural tools is made possible if they themselves are conceived as types of activities (see Stetsenko, 1999). Indeed, cultural tools cannot be reduced to being mere objects or things but should be conceptualized instead as embodiments of certain cultural practices, as crystallized templates of action and schematized representations of ways of doing things as discovered in the history of human civilization. Cultural tools are, in this sense, embodiments of the function and meaning of sociocultural practices; they are "objects that can be used for certain purpose" in the human community. As such, they can be appropriated by the child only by acting upon and with them, only in the course of actively reconstructing their meaning and function.

Such reconstructions of cultural tools are initially possible only in the process of cooperation and interaction with other people who already possess the knowledge (and, hence, the meaning) of a given cultural tool. In this sense, it is through social interaction that cultural tools are provided to children, and this is precisely why all human activities can be said to be socioculturally determined and situated. In this perspective, cultural tools are never something merely added from outside to the child's mind; neither are they structural characteristics of the developing mind. Given that the developing mind is as an essentially sociocultural activity that is always geared to specifically human conjoint purposes and goals, the mastery of cultural tools and, hence, of the culturally appropriate ways to attain these goals becomes a major pathway for human development (for details, see Arievitch & Stetsenko, 2000).

It is this pathway that ultimately defines the very fabric and texture of human mind. In addition, mastery of cultural tools always occurs in unique circumstances that typify each child's situation of development, and children themselves play an active agentic role in this process. That is why children's understanding, gained while mastering cultural tools in collaboration with others, always incorporates an amalgam of individual, sociocultural, and historical properties of knowledge. That is also why individuals never become dissolved in the linguistic or social reality of interaction.

This last implication about cultural tools as practices through which children are introduced into the ways of acting in sociocultural reality and, hence, also into the ways of knowing this reality is empirically addressed by Bearison and Dorval through their emphasis on how children use language and speech in collaborative problem solving. They explore not simply how children talk to express their ideas for purely communicative purposes but also the ways that language is used as a cultural tool to distance them from the immediacy of their pragmatic interests and desires and, thereby, to promote the development of abstract modes of reasoning and representation. In other words, children's discourse is viewed as a tool of a larger pragmatic sociocultural activity—in this case, the collaborative activity of constructing rules for a board game. Language, in this sense, is not withdrawn from a real-life process as some independent (i.e., purely expressive) superstructure but is reintegrated with social relations and practices to form a functional whole.

This is a clear contrast to a purely discourse-oriented approach in which discourse processes are abstracted from the reality of practical activity to become a dominant structure that exists on its own grounds, develops according to its own rules, and, moreover, entails the human mind, the self, and other traditional psychological constructs as epiphenomenal by-products (e.g., Gergen, 1994; Harré, 1987).

In general then, the three interrelated implications taken together suggest that there is more to the social collaborative nature of the human mind than is commonly assumed in much of mainstream research that strives to add some social components to its individual-oriented methodology. That the mind is social means not only that people often act together and use cultural artifacts to make their mental processes more efficient. It also means that the very "nature" of the human mind is conceived in a completely new way in regard to very concrete aspects, such as where it is thought to be located, where it "starts and where it ends," how it is constituted, and how it develops.

That the human mind is social means that it is a real-time process of practical transformative activities (and, hence, located outside of the head!) aimed at solving specifically human, collaborative types of problems with the help of sociocultural means that have been developed in the history of civilization within specific cultural contexts. The human mind, conceived of as such a real-time process with its own dynamic is never preprogrammed in the blueprints of genes or environmental influences and prepackaged in some mental states or attributes. On the contrary, it is an emergent reality created within the flow and from the cycles of collaborative, specifically human, activities mediated by sociocultural artifacts. This process stands between nature and nurture. The sociocultural reality taken as a sociocultural collaborative practice of conjoint problem solving, then, is not just an addition to the otherwise solipsistic notion of individual development and not just the context within which the development of mind takes place. Rather, this sociocultural collaborative practice of conjoint problem solving is the very stuff and substance that human development is made from. In other words, the human mind is understood as a dynamic process that is constructed each time anew as it "comes into being through doing," where doing is a sociocultural collaborative practice aimed at sociocultural goals and purposes. That is why a researcher who assumes this perspective never looks at relationships per se between autonomous individuals (even if this relationship is expressed in discursive form) but at the ways in which the mind comes to be constituted through particular collaborative activities, including activities of a discursive type.

As Bearison and Dorval acknowledge, a certain affinity exists between this sociocultural view of human mind, on the one hand, and the dynamic systems approach developed by Nikolaj A. Bernstein (a Russian contemporary of Lev S. Vygotsky) and elaborated by E. Thelen and her collaborators (e.g., Thelen & Smith, 1994), on the other. According to this latter approach, however, higher order mental activities, including categorization, concept formation, and language arise in a self-organized manner from the recurrent real-time activities of an individual child, whereas the role of cultural tools and the whole sociocultural dimension of this development is not in the focus of attention (for a comparison of activity theory and dynamic systems approach, see Jones, 1999).

Bearison and Dorval's research strategy is congruent with and can be viewed as a means of operationalizing the theoretical premises formulated above. It is in direct congruence with these premises that their focus is on how children cognitively participate in social and cultural activities and less on the ways in which culture and society affect children's individual cognitive development. It is in direct congruence with these premises that the relative contributions of participants in a dyad are considered as emergent and transformative of each other's ideas and ways of reasoning rather than being simply additive and accumulative. Their research is also in direct congruence (cf. Bearison & Dorval, p. 88) with the central role accorded by Vygotsky to culturally mediated discourse and by Piaget to joint coordinations of actions (i.e., through decentrations as they arise from mutually conflicting interpersonal centrations) in the development of thought.

Their focus is on activities that require children to make sense of situations in order to fulfill some culturally prescribed pragmatic purpose, namely, to co-construct their own rules for a board game. In other words, the unit of analyses is the pattern of collaborative discourse among peers that serves as a means of negotiating task resolutions and achieving higher levels of game complexity. Hence, mutual understanding is not regarded as some kind of an abstract goal that collaborating peers strive to achieve but rather a practical means of solving a concrete real task of developing rules for a board game. Because both interactions and the resulting qualities of the board games were analyzed, the conceptual boundaries between ways of interacting, on the one hand, and cognitive outcomes, on the other, might have been confounded in the process (cf. Bearison & Dorval, p. 16). However, Bearison and Dorval managed to find ways of looking into a complex dynamic system that entailed both the patterns of discourse and the game rules with increasing levels of complexity resulting from collaborative interaction. According to Bearison and Dorval, it is this system that represents the evolving social mind of children participating in collaborative activities, and it is this system that replaces individual minds as the central object of inquiry.

Therefore, what Bearison and Dorval offer is a research strategy that puts to test the collaborative mind without treating it as a "black box." Instead, on the one hand, shared engagements in collaborative activities are analyzed from the point of view of their content (what is talked about) and mode (how these contents are expressed), and, on the other hand, the increasing levels of game complexity are analyzed in terms of their logical composition and in conjunction with the type of negotiating strategies that children use. A sophisticated method of analyzing these collaborative processes—microanalytic dialogical analyses of interaction in a relatively informal and open-ended situation of constructing rules for a board game—served well the general purposes and theoretical orientation of their study.

It is not surprising, then, that the specific findings of their study directly speak to the dynamics inherent in this system of collaborative activities entailing both the patterns of discourse and the game rules with increasing levels of complexity. For example, the process of co-constructing complex games has been found to be merged with the process of coordinating perspectives between the participants. When participants cognitively operated on and transformed each other's ideas, it was considered a kind of "interactive logic" (or expansive kind of negotiations), and it is in this kind of reasoning upon the reasoning of another that more and more complex game rules emerged. In other words, the key to achieving high levels of co-constructive mastery in collaborative cognition was found in the quality of negotiations leading to games of higher complexity. Specifically, the more children were able to generate a relatively high proportion of expansive kinds of negotiations (i.e., negotiations involving turns by which participants augmented their partner's game proposals) and to avoid unresolved kinds of negotiations, the more logically complex rules for their board games were generated in this process. Thus, the sequential patterns of discourse representing a continuum of developmental change from less to more complex kinds of cognition have been dynamically defined and operationalized.

In general, the approach taken by Bearison and Dorval benefits from both the Vygotskian and the Piagetian lines of thought and combines them in a creative and fruitful way, making progress in ways of studying the social collaborative mind. This progress relative to Piaget, for example, is that mathematical formalisms in and of themselves are not believed anymore to capture structures of thought. Whereas for Piaget, knowledge structures were formalizations of the structure of the tasks he used, for Bearison and Dorval, knowledge structures necessarily have to be the formalizations of psychological processes—processes that entail narratives that serve the purpose of developing knowledge (of board game rules, in this case) at increasingly complex and abstract levels. This is an important shift of perspective since it prioritizes psychological ways of analyses over purely logical ones. And relative to Vygotsky, as described throughout this commentary, their progress can be seen in that the general implications of his sociocultural theory are methodologically explored in research that takes sociocultural events as its unit of analysis.

Appendix:
The Coding Manual

OUTLINE OF PEER INTERACTION AND GAME CONSTRUCTION CODES

I. Conversational Turns

Functions

1. initial proposal
2. counterproposal
3. disagreement
4. agreement
5. elicitation
6. repetition
7. demonstration
8. elaboration
9. qualification
10. compromise

11. confirmation request
12. ignore or an aside
13. clarification

Justifications

1. Unjustified
2. Factually justified
3. Perspectively justified

II. Negotiation Episodes

Kinds of Negotiations

1. Ignored
2. Unresolved
3. Withdrawn
4. Acquiescence
5. Acceptance of proposal
6. Expansive
7. Compromise
8. Synthesis

Game Topics

1. Designation Rules
2. Procedural Rules
3. Conditional Rules
4. Constraining Rules
5. Goals

Joint Planning

1. Planning
2. Active

III. Game Complexity Components per Episode

Change Indicators

0. No change
1. Change up
2. Change down

Change Components

0. No change
1. First designation or procedural rule
2. First conditional rule
3. First explicit goal
4. First system of scoring
5. First additional goal
6. Every constraining rule
7. Every complex conditional rule
8. Every rule for alternative pathway
9. Every goal for alternative pathway

Backward Pathway

0. No
1. Yes

Evolving Levels of Complexity

Continuing sequence of numbers of complexity levels

COMBINED PEER INTERACTION CODES

I. Conversational Turns

Functions

1. initial proposal

2. counterproposal
3. disagreement
4. agreement
5. elicitation
6. repetition
7. elaboration (qualification, compromise)
8. confirmation request
9. ignore or an aside
10. clarification (demonstration)

Justifications

1. Unjustified
2. Justified (factually, perspectively)

II. Negotiation Episodes

Kinds of Negotiations

1. Unresolved (ignored, withdrawn)
2. Acquiescence
3. Acceptance of proposal
4. Expansive (compromise, synthesis)

GENERAL CONSIDERATIONS

Conversational Turns

A conversational turn begins from the time a speaker begins talking and ends when he or she stops talking (excluding interruptions by the other speaker, unless the first explicitly responds to the interruption).

Two or more conversational turns constitute a **negotiation strategy**, where the initial turn typically is an "initial proposal" but can also be an "elicitation." Exceptions in which a negotiation consists of only one conversational turn are cases in which one partner accepts the initial proposal of the other partner by gestures rather than verbal conversation, and in those cases the gesture will be coded as a conversational turn.

A conversational turn must consist minimally of a subject and a predicate or an implied predicate (i.e., incomplete utterances are not coded). In rare instances a turn may consist of a nonverbal gesture (e.g., one partner picking up a particular piece when asked by the other partner which piece he or she wants to use).

In special conditions in which two functionally distinct statements are included within a single conversational turn, they should be separately coded with the same conversational turn assignment.

Prompts by one partner for the other to continue conversing are not coded, and the other partner's continuation is counted as part of his or her original turn.

Negotiation Strategies

Every negotiation strategy must contain at least one proposal.

Negotiation strategies are distinguished from "activity speech," which is not coded as it does not refer to generalized proposals but reflects the game playing activity. An example of "activity speech" is A: "I have to go first . . . I have to go again. OK? [has landed on the line on the spinner]"

Arguments between partners about methods of play established by preexisting negotiated rules and/or goals are not considered negotiations unless they change preexisting rules or goals (i.e., renegotiations).

Labeling—Simply identifying the pieces without verbally considering whether they will be used in a game is considered a label and not a proposal. If partners negotiate the identity of a piece without considering its use, then it's not a proposal.

Designators—The following pieces can be used as designators: dice, colored cube, numbered cards, paper money, spinner, paper and pencil. Statements about where they should be physically placed when they are used as designators does not count as a proposal. For example, "Put the spinner over there" is not counted as a proposal, but "Each pile of the money goes on a different color of the spinner" is counted as a proposal.

A negotiation strategy begins when one partner proposes one or more rules, goals, or uses of materials or a change(s) in existing rules, goals or materials, and continues through successive conversational turns until the initial proposal and its derivatives are no longer a topic of discourse. A negotiation strategy also can begin with an elicitation for a proposal. Topics are operationally defined according to the five categories of game topics: designation rules, conditional rules, constraining rules, procedural rules, and goals. But note that the conversational turn that changes the topic is not counted as the last turn in the negotiation, but the immediately previous conversational turn is. In some cases, a second negotiation might begin within a single conversational turn when, in such a conversational turn, there is a change of topic.

Conversational turns that occur in order to set up a subsequent proposal are not included as part of a negotiation strategy (e.g., "Oh, I have an idea").

In cases where dyads end playing a given game and then begin a new game, the negotiation episode number resorts to "one" for the first negotiation of the new game, but the turn number continues to increase; the game complexity score reverts back to zero and subsequent coding reflects the increasing complexity of the new game.

CODE DEFINITIONS

I. Conversational Turns

A. Conversational Turn Functions

1. initial proposal—a statement describing a *generalized* method of play or designation of a goal. Note that a negotiation need not begin with an initial proposal. It can begin with an elicitation. Note that an initial proposal can be worded sometimes as a question but not coded as an elicitation (e.g., "Should we use both black dogs?"; "Two players, all right?").

> EX 1: "Let's place the red chip here, so we know it's the start." (*initial proposal*)
>
> EX 2: "The first one that gets to the center wins." (*initial proposal*)

2. counterproposal—a disagreement with a preceding proposal within the negotiation strategy together with a substitute proposal.

> EX 1: A: "We'll use the green for a special space."
>
> B: "No, how 'bout like this? With blue and yellow, you get green." (*counterproposal*)
>
> EX 2: A: "It's the fishes who get to start."
>
> B: "No, the robot gets to start." (*counterproposal*)
>
> EX 3: A: "You have to go down this one, and then you have to come all the way up here."
>
> B: "No, you have to go down that way [opposite direction from A's proposal]." (*counterproposal*)

3. disagreement—a disagreement with (1) a previously expressed proposal within the negotiation strategy, or (2) with the partner's statement or enactment in an immediately previous turn.

> EX 1: A: "If you spin gold once, you get a fish."
>
> B: "No, actually we shouldn't use these guys." (*disagreement*)
>
> EX 2: A: "The fish should give us one point. We get one point for killing that."
>
> B: "No, I don't think we should." (*disagreement*)

A: "Yeah, cause it's hard to kill a fish." (*disagreement*)
B: "No, it's not." (*disagreement*)

4. agreement—agreement with a previously expressed proposal within the negotiation strategy (either expressed verbally and/or enacted by gesture [e.g., shaking head affirmatively]).

EX 1: A: "Okay, yeah, mm-hmm" (*agreement*)
EX 2: A: "Let's see if it's enough. One, two, three . . ."
     B: "It's exactly enough to get across the board."
     (*agreement*)

5. elicitation—a request for further information about a proposal.

If an elicitation for agreement occurs in a conversational turn in which another code is marked, the elicitation is not coded. If the sole function of the elicitation is for one partner to elicit from the other an agreement, then it's coded as a "confirmation request" and not an elicitation.

EX 1: "Well, what's this for?" (*elicitation*)
EX 2: "Who goes first?" (*elicitation*)

6. repetition—a repetition, although not necessarily literal, of a previously expressed proposal, counterproposal, demonstration, elaboration, qualification, or compromise within the negotiation strategy.

When the repetition is of a form other than those listed above, (e.g., another request for more information) it is coded as a new occurrence of that form and not as a repetition.

EX 1: A: "That's your ten. You're the banker."
     B: "No, no, you give me all the rest of the money over there."
     A: "Yeah, but you're the banker." (*repetition*)

EX 2: A: "Yeah, you have to get the same puppy on the same (space), like the puppies haveto match."
B: "Yeah, the puppies have to match." (*repetition*)

7. demonstration—a presentation by one partner of how a proposal would function.

EX 1: A: "I think it should be behind where you came. So how did you come?"
B: "I went like that." (*demonstration*)

EX 2: A: "I can go wherever I want. You can go like that or like that. You can go 1, 2, 3, 4, 5." (*demonstrates movement of marker on the board*)

8. elaboration—1. a partner augments the other's proposal about conditions of the game being constructed. 2. A partner completes the thoughts of the other by adding/completing a compatible rule, goal or justification to a proposal.

EX 1: A: "When you get the gold you can kill the fish and you get more."
B: "You can shoot the fish." (*elaboration*)
A: "Because both guys have guns."
B: "And then you get teleported to the fishy . . . and then it goes into the fishy graveyard, right?" (*elaboration*)

EX 2: A: "When we play, we go like this. You start from here, and I'll start from here and . . ."
B: "Yeah, and whoever gets to this first, wins." (*elaboration*)

9. qualification—restricting or constraining the conditions of deployment on the partner's or the self's previously expressed proposal.

EX 1: A: "You can move the guys out."
  B: "You're only supposed to when you zap a fish."
  (*qualification*)
EX 2: A: "You're gonna eat a bug, right?"
  B: "Only if I get a red."(*qualification*)

10. compromise—a suggestion by one partner of a way to reconcile a disagreement in progress by integrating aspects of the opposing positions.

EX: [A: "I'll be these two robots."] note: not part of the
  negotiation
  B: "I'll be these four dogs, and my four dogs are here.
  You get to move one thing at a time."
  A: "You only get two things at a time because there
  are only two robots." (*disagreement*)
  B: "You can get two more things." (*compromise*)

11. confirmation request—a question by one partner concerning whether the other partner agrees with his or her statement.

EX 1: "So, do you agree with that?"
EX 2: "Okay, I'll be the banker. Do you want me to be the
  banker?"

12. ignore or an aside—one or more statements by one partner that are non responsive to the topic of the other partner's proposal (or elicitation).

EX. Ignore: A: "The first one to get here is the winner."
  B: *"One, two, three, four (moving his piece)"* (*ignore*)
  A: "The first one to get there is the winner, but
  the other player will try to bam you back."

EX. Aside: A: "Let's move the robot to the center if you get
a blue."
B: "Look, it's snowing outside."(*aside*)

13. clarification—an explanation offered by one partner regarding the meaning of a proposal that doesn't alter (or expand)
its conditions of deployment. A clarification often appears as a
response to an elicitation, but it not need do so.

EX 1: A: "We have to pay for the dogs."
B: "What are the dogs worth?"
A: "Five hundred dollars" (*clarification*)
EX 2: A: "Yellow is worth the most."
B: "Yeah, why?"
A: "Because there's a few blacks and less yellows."
(*clarification*)

Conversational turns that are not coded within negotiation sequences
1. **Interruptions**—Interruptions (and asides) are off-nego-
tiation discourse that occurs within a negotiation sequence. They
occur when one person interrupts the discourse of the other with
unrelated talk and without interrupting the topic of the previous
person's discourse and who continues talking. The interruption
will not be entered in the coding scheme and both parts of the
other speaker's discourse which was intruded upon will be
coded as a single conversational turn.
In following examples, both parts of A's discourse will be
coded as a single proposal.

EX 1: A: "Maybe also what we could do . . ."
B: "Oh no!" (*not coded*)
A: ". . . is instead of these having to be for money, for
going on that gray, you could get acertain number
of blue chips."
EX 2: A: "And if you go to the blue you get . . ."
B: "What are these, they have numbers?" (*not coded*)
A: "You get a hundred dollars."

B. Justification

1. **Unjustified**

EX: A: "And use the red one here."
    B: "No, the grey and the brown and the light green."
    (*unjustified*)

2. **Factually justified**—justification in terms of the methods of play. Justifications always refer to one's own statement that's being justified.

EX 1: continued from the negotiation from above example . . .
    " 'Cause those are the ones we don't have." (*factually justified*)

EX 2: "Let's take money, *'cause money's good* "(*factually justified*)

EX 3: "No, it's not. Well not really. I don't think we should because that's not like the object of the game. The object of the game is to kill all the fish and get the treasures." (*factually justified*)

3. **Perspectively justified**—justifies own position by making reference to self's and/or other's perspective (i.e., thoughts, feelings, intentions, and/or behavior).

EX 1: "I never get a chance to make up a rule." (*perspectively justified*)

EX 2: "Yea! Well that's the way I want it to be." (*perspectively justified*)

EX 3: "No, George. You can't make up all the rules" (*perspectively justified*)

II. Negotiation Episodes

A. Types of Negotiation Strategies

1. Ignored. One partner changes the topic of discourse without responding to or recognizing one or more proposals offered by the other partner.

2. Unresolved. One partner changes the topic of discourse without reconciling one or more contested proposals (i.e., without having achieved either a compromise, acquiescence, or synthesis).

3. Withdrawn. One partner withdraws his or her proposal without a counter- or compromise proposal in reaction to objections expressed by the other partner.

4. Acquiescence. One partner *passively* accepts the other partner's proposal (without elaboration) by expressing something like, "Yeah," or "OK," or by enacting the proposal at the next turn.

5. Acceptance of proposal. One partner accepts the other's proposal after actively considering it in the form of either an unacceptable proposal, a counterproposal, a repetition, a disagreement, or a verification.

6. Expansive. One partner accepted the other's proposal but only after having added new conditions to it, or having offered a counterproposal that was unconditionally accepted by the other.

7. Compromise. One partner adjusts the other's proposal by incorporating the conflicting claims or disagreements that he or she had with the other's proposal (i.e., a settlement of differences by mutual concessions).

8. Synthesis. One partner resolves differences between his or her own proposal and the other's proposal by incorporating or logically integrating aspects of each of their preceding and conflicting proposals.

B. Game Topic

Game topics refer to the function of the negotiated proposals as they establish new rules or goals or affect existing rules or goals. Rule refer to methods of play (i.e., the "how" of playing) and a goals refer to the purpose or object of play (i.e., the "why" of playing).

Note that negotiation strategies of the kind (1) ignored, (2) unresolved, or (3) withdrawn have game topic codes without change indicator codes and level of game complexity codes.

1. Designation rules specify labels of pieces, values attributed to pieces, and their places on the board.

EX: "This is the place where we keep the money."

2. Procedural rules designate procedures or methods of play (in terms of moving pieces on the board).

EX: "You have to roll the dice to see how much you get to go."

3. Conditional rules imply or state "if/then" relationships between game conditions and procedures of play.

EX: "If you get to the blue, then you get five dollars."

4. Constraining rules create parameters of play (boundaries, constraints) that did not exist before and within which other preexisting rules must now operate.

EX: "If you get anything besides green, you have to go there until you get a green."

5. Goals (and subgoals) designate the object or purpose of the game or, in the case of subgoals, some part of the game.

EX: "We move and the first one to get to the center wins."

C. Joint Planning

This set of codes was intended to reflect whether partners used planning outside the context of actually enacting their methods of game playing when negotiating and whether that occurred in anticipation of the enactment. Use of planning types of negotiations, compared to active negotiations, were expected to be associated with several kinds of discourse and game level complexity.

Planned negotiations: Negotiation strategies that were not prompted by nor incurred during the act of playing the game.

Embedded negotiations: Negotiation strategies that were directly prompted by game activities and, therefore, were initiated when participants were playing parts of the game they were co-constructing.

III. Game Complexity

A. Change Indicator

0. No change.

1. Change up. The negotiation strategy has the effect of increasing the level of game complexity by one or more factors.

2. Change down. The negotiation strategy has the effect of decreasing the level of game complexity by one or more factors.

B. Components Determining Levels of Game Complexity

When a given negotiation sequence involves more than one change component, choose the higher numbered code. Components 1 through 5 refer to "the first introduction" and components 6 through 9, to "each occurrence" of some rule or goal.

  0. No change.

1. The first introduction of a **designation rule or procedural rule** without explicitly stating a goal.

2. The first introduction of a **conditional rule** (that doesn't provide an additional pathway).

3. The first introduction of an **explicit goal** (i.e., win statement).

> EX 1: "Whoever gets to the center and has the most money wins the game."
>
> EX 2: "Whoever gets to the center wins the game."

4. The first introduction of a **system of scoring** in terms of procedures and goals (usually will be a kind of procedural rule).

5. The first introduction of an **additional goal** that creates a new ultimate goal increases the game complexity. (The first goal becomes a condition for then achieving the [new] ultimate goal).

6. Every occurrence of a **constraining rule** that complicates the achievement of a goal increases the game level complexity.

7. Every occurrence of a **complex conditional rule**. A complex conditional rule is a rule in which more than one if-then type of condition is specified.

A conditional rule takes into account the history of play and operates on the outcome of a given player's achievement of a previous condition in the game rather than on a game ascription. In a simple conditional rule, the givens are constants and in a complex conditional rule, the status of the game conditions are variable.

> EX: "If he touches you when you're dead, you can go back to life, but if he touches you when you're still living, you get more life."

8. Every occurrence of a **rule for an alternative pathway** that establishes an additional (i.e., alternative) pathway to a given or new goal (can occur indefinitely by adding on components). What's a *pathway*? It is an alternative procedure for achieving a goal.

> EX: A: "If you want, you can give all your money in, and then you can get out."

B: "How much?"

A: "Five hundred dollars. Otherwise you have to wait
a turn and have to get the dog rescuer."

9. Every occurrence of a **goal for alternative pathways** that
establishes an additional (i.e., alternative) pathway to a given or
new goal (can occur indefinitely by adding on components).

C. Backward Pathway

0. No change components within the strategy had the effect
of creating a backward pathway in the game structure.

1. One or more change components within the strategy had
the effect of creating a backward pathway in the game structure.
A backward pathway is created by a rule that causes a reversal
in the forward movement of pieces toward a goal, or the loss of
items needed to attain a goal.

D. Evolving Levels of Complexity

This is a number sequenced from 1 onwards that indicates the
current level of game complexity at the end of any given strategy.

References

Ames, G., & Murray, F. (1982). When two wrongs make a right: Promoting cognitive change by social conflict. *Developmental Psychology*, 18, 894–897.

Arievitch, I., & van der Veer, R. (1995). Furthering the internalization debate: Gal'perin's contribution. *Human Development*, 38, 1132–1126.

Arievitch, I. M., & Stetsenko, A. (2000). Development through learning: Gal'perin's contribution. *Human Development*, 43, 69–93.

Azmitia, M. (1988). Peer interaction and problem solving: When two heads are better than one? *Child Development*, 59, 87–96.

Azmitia, M., & Montgomery, R. (1993). Friendship, transactive dialogues, and the development of scientific reasoning. *Social Development*, 2, 202–221.

Bakeman, R., Adamson, L. B., Strisik, P. (1989). Lags and logs: Statistical approaches to interaction. In M. Bornstein & J. Bruner (Eds.), *Interactions in human development.* (pp. 244–260). Hillsdale, NJ: Erlbaum.

Bakeman, R., & Brownlee, J. R. (1980). The strategic use of parallel play. *Child Development*, 51, 873–878.

Bakeman, R., & Gottman, J. M. (1986). *Observing interaction: An introduction to sequential analysis.* Cambridge: Cambridge University Press.

Bakeman, R., & Quera, V. (1995a). *Analyzing interaction: Sequential analysis with SDIS and GSEQ.* New York: Cambridge University Press.

Bakeman, R., & Quera, V. (1995b). Log-linear approaches to lag-sequential analysis when consecutive codes may and cannot repeat. *Psychological Bulletin*, 118, 272–284.

Bakeman, R., & Robinson, B. F. (1994). *Understanding log-linear analysis with ILOG: An interactive approach.* Hillsdale, NJ: Erlbaum.

Bakeman, R., Robinson, B. F., & Quera, V. (1996). Testing sequential association: Estimating exact p values using sampling permutations. *Psychological Methods*, 1, 4–15.

Bakhtin, M. M. (1981). *The dialogical imagination: Four essays by M. M. Bakhtin* (M. Holquist, Ed.). Austin: University of Texas Press.

Bakhtin, M. M. (1986). *Speech genres and other late essays* (C. Emerson & M. Holquist, Eds.). Austin: University of Texas Press.

Bearison, D. J. (1969). The role of measurement operations in the acquisition of conservation. *Developmental Psychology*, 1, 653–660.

Bearison, D. J. (1982). New directions in studies of social interaction and cognitive growth. In F. Serafica (Ed.), *Social cognitive development in context* (pp. 199–221). New York: Guilford Press.

Bearison, D. J. (1983). Who killed the epistemic subject? In W. Overton (Ed.), *The relationship between social and cognitive development.* Hillsdale, NJ: Erlbaum.

Bearison, D. J. (1986). Transactional cognition in context: New models of social understanding. In D. Bearison & H. Zimiles (Eds.), *Thought and emotion: Developmental perspectives* (pp. 129–146). Hillsdale, NJ: Erlbaum.

Bearison, D. J. (1991). Interactional contexts of cognitive development: Piagetian approaches to sociogenesis. In L. T. Landsmann (Ed.), *Culture, cognition and schooling* (pp. 56–70). Norwood, NJ: Ablex.

Bearison, D. J., Magzamen, S., & Filardo, E. (1986). Sociocognitive conflict and cognitive growth in young children. *Merrill-Palmer Quarterly, 32,* 51–72.

Berkowitz, M. W., & Gibbs, J. C. (1983). Measuring the development of features of moral discussion. *Merrill-Palmer Quarterly, 29,* 399–410.

Brenneis, D. (1988). Language and disputing. *American Review of Anthropology, 17,* 221–237.

Broughton, J. M. (1982). Cognitive interaction and the development of sociality. *Merrill-Palmer Quarterly, 28,* 369–378.

Brown, A. L., & Palincsar, A. S. (1989). Guided, cooperative learning and individual knowledge acquisition. In L. B. Resnick (Ed.), *Knowing, learning, and instruction.* Hillsdale, NJ: Erlbaum.

Bruner, J. S., & Bornstein, M. H. (1989). On interaction. In M. H. Bornstein & J. S. Bruner (Eds.), *Interaction in human development* (pp. 1–16). Hillsdale, NJ: Erlbaum.

Caplan, P. J., Crawford, M., Hyde, J. S., & Richardson. J. T. E. (1997). *Gender differences in human cognition.* New York: Oxford University Press.

Chapman, M. (1989). *Constructive evolution.* Cambridge: Cambridge University Press.

Chapman, M., & McBride, M. L. (1992). The education of reason: Cognitive conflict and its role in intellectual development. In C. U. Shantz & W. Hartup (Eds.), *Conflict in child and adolescent development* (pp. 36–69). Cambridge: Cambridge University Press.

Cocking, R., & Renninger, A. (Eds.). (1993). *The development and meaning of psychological distance.* Hillsdale, NJ: Erlbaum.

Cole, M. (1981). *The zone of proximal development: Where culture and cognition create each other* (Report No. 106, September).

San Diego: University of California San Diego, Center for Human Information Processing.

Cole, M., & Wertsch, J. V. (1996). Beyond the individual-social antinomy in discussions of Piaget and Vygotsky. *Human Development, 39*, 250–256.

Cooney, E. (1977). *Application of an elementary grade social cognitive intervention.* Unpublished doctoral dissertation, Harvard University.

Crook, C. (1994). *Computers and the collaborative experience of learning.* London: Routledge.

Csikszentmihalyi, M., & Rathunde, K. (1998). In W. Damon (Gen. Ed.) & R. Lerner (Ed.), *Handbook of child psychology: Vol. 1. Theoretical models of human development* (pp. 635–684). New York: Wiley.

Damon, W. (1983). The nature of social-cognitive change in the developing child. In W. Overton (Ed.), *The relationship between social and cognitive development.* Hillsdale, NJ: Erlbaum.

Damon, W. (1991). Problems of direction in socially shared cognition. In L. B. Resnick, J. M. Levine, & S. D. Teasley, (Eds.), *Perspectives on socially shared cognition* (pp. 384–397). Washington, DC: American Psychological Association.

Damon, W. (1994). Commentary on Verba, M. The beginnings of collaboration in peer interaction. *Human Development, 37,* 140–142.

Damon, W., & Killen, M. (1982). Peer interaction and the process of change in children's moral reasoning. *Merrill-Palmer Quarterly, 28,* 347–367.

Dimant, R. J., & Bearison, D. J. (1991).The development of formal reasoning during successive peer interactions. *Developmental Psychology, 27,* 277–284.

Doise, W., & Mugny, G. (1984). *The social development of the intellect.* Oxford: Pergamon Press.

Dorval, B. (1999). A Bakhtinian view of egocentric speech. In I. Sigel (Ed.), *Theories of representation.* Mahwah, NJ: Erlbaum.

Dorval, B., & Eckerman, C. O. (1984). Developmental trends in the quality of conversation achieved by small groups of acquainted peers. *Monographs of the Society for Research in Child Development*, (Serial No. 26).

Dorval, B., & Gundy, F. (1990). The development of arguing in discussions among peers. *Merrill-Palmer Quarterly, 36*, 389–409.

Duran, R. T., & Gauvain, M. (1993). The role of age versus expertise in peer collaboration during joint planning. *Journal of Experimental Child Psychology, 55*, 227–242.

Durkheim, E. (1925/1973). *Moral education*. New York: Free Press.

Eiferman, R. R. (1971). Social play in childhood. In R. E. Herron & B. Sutton-Smith (Eds.), *Child's play*. New York: Wiley.

Eisenberg, A. R., & Garvey, C. (1981). Children's use of verbal strategies in resolving conflicts. *Discourse Processes, 4*, 149–170.

Ellis, S., & Gauvain, M. (1992). Social and cultural influences on children's collaborative interactions. In L. T. Winegar & J. Valsiner (Eds.), *Children's development within social contexts* (pp. 155–180). Hillsdale, NJ: Erlbaum.

Ellis, S., Klahr, D., & Siegler, R. S. (1994, April). The birth, life, and sometimes death of good ideas in collaborative problem solving. Paper presented at the meetings of the American Educational Research Association, New Orleans, AL.

Ellis, S., & Rogoff, B. (1986). Problem solving in children's management of instruction. In E. Mueller & C. Cooper (Eds.), *Process and outcome in peer relationships* (pp. 301–325). Orlando, FL: Academic Press.

Emler, N., & Valiant, G. L. (1982). Social interaction and cognitive conflict in the development of spatial coordination skills. *British Journal of Psychology, 73*, 295–303.

Enright, R. (1976). *An experimental analysis of a social cognitive model through a cross-age training program*. Unpublished doctoral dissertation, University of Minnesota.

Flavell, J. H. (1977). *Cognitive development*. Englewood Cliffs, NJ: Prentice-Hall.

Forman, E. A., & Kraker, M. J. (1985). The social origins of logic: The contributions of Piaget and Vygotsky. In M. Berkowitz (Ed.), *Peer conflict and psychological growth* (pp. 23–39). San Francisco: Jossey-Bass.

Friedman, S. L., & Scholnick, E. K. (Eds.). (1997). *The developmental psychology of planning: Why, how, and when do we plan?* Mahwah, NJ: Erlbaum.

Furth, H. (1968). The nature of representation and interiorization. *Psychological Review, 5*, 143–154.

Garvey, C. (1986). Peer relations and the growth of communication. In E. C. Muller & C. R. Cooper (Eds.), *Process and outcome in peer relations* (pp. 329–345). Orlando, FL: Academic Press.

Garvey, C., & Shantz, C. U. (1992). Conflict talk: Approaches to adversative discourse. In C. U. Shantz & W. Hartup (Eds.), *Conflict in child and adolescent development* (pp. 93–121). Cambridge, MA: Cambridge University Press.

Gauvain, M., & Rogoff, B. (1989). Collaborative problem solving and children's planning skills. *Developmental Psychology, 25*, 139–151.

Glachan, M., & Light, P. (1982). Peer interaction and learning: Can two wrongs make a right? In G. Butterworth & P. Light (Eds.), *Social cognition: Studies of the development of understanding* (pp. 238–262). Brighton, UK: Harvester Press.

Goodnow, J. J. (1997). The interpersonal and social aspects of planning. In S. L. Friedman & E. K. Scholnick (Eds.), *The developmental psychology of planning: Why, how, and when do we plan?* (pp. 339–358). Mahwah, NJ: Erlbaum.

Gottman, J. M. (1979). Deducting cyclicity in social interaction. *Psychological Bulletin, 86*, 338–348.

Habermas, J. (1984). *The theory of communicative action: Vol 1. Reason and the rationalization of society.* Boston: Beacon Press.

Harris, J. R. (1995). Where is the child's environment? A group socialization theory of development. *Psychological Review, 102*, 458–489.

Hartup, W. W. (1985). Relationships and their significance in cognitive development. In R. Hinde & A. Perret-Clermont (Eds.), *Relationships and cognitive development* (pp. 66–82). Oxford: Oxford University Press.

Hartup, W. W. (1992). Conflict and friendship relations. In C. U. Shantz & W. Hartup (Eds.), *Conflict in child and adolescent development* (pp. 186–215). Cambridge: Cambridge University Press.

Hartup, W. W., French, D. C., Laursen, B., Johnston, M. K., & Ogawa, J. R. (1993). Conflict and friendship relations in middle childhood: Behavior in a closed-field situation. *Child Development, 64,* 445–454.

Hawking, J. (1987, April). Collaboration and dissent. Paper presented at the meetings of the Society for Research in Child Development, Baltimore, MD.

Inhelder, B., Sinclair, H., & Bovet, M. (1974). *Learning and the development of cognition.* London: Routledge & Kegan Paul.

Johnson, D. W., & Johnson, R. T. (1987). *Learning together and alone: Cooperative, competitive and individualistic learning* (2nd ed.). Englewood Cliffs, NJ: Prentice-Hall.

Kaplan, B. (October, 1974). *Rationality and irrationality in development: Strife of systems.* Heinz Werner Memorial Lecture, Clark University, Worcester, MA

Kitchener, R. F. (1996). The nature of the social for Piaget and Vygotsky. *Human Development, 39,* 243–249.

Kruger, A. C. (1992). The effect of peer and adult-child transactive discussions on moral reasoning. *Merrill-Palmer Quarterly, 38,* 191–211.

Kruger, A. C., & Tomasello, M. (1986). Transactive discussions with peers and adults. *Developmental Psychology, 22,* 681–685.

Kuhn, D. (1972). Mechanisms of change in the development of cognitive structures. *Child Development, 43,* 833–842.

Lawrence, J. A., & Valsiner, J. (1993). Conceptual roots of internalization: From transmission to transformation. *Human Development, 36,* 150–167.

LeBlanc, G., & Bearison, D. J. (1997, April). *The shift in roles in the expert-novice dyad.* Paper presented at the meeting of the Society for Research in Child Development, Washington, DC.

Leont'ev, A. N. (1978). *Activity, consciousness and personality.* Englewood Cliffs, NJ: Prentice Hall.

Leont'ev, A. N. (1981). The problem of activity in psychology. In J. V. Wertsch (Ed.), *The concept of activity in Soviet psychology* (pp. 37–71). Armonk, NY: Sharpe.

Levin, I., & Druyan, S. (1993). When sociocognitive transaction among peers fails: The case of misconceptions in science. *Child Development, 64,* 1671–1691.

Lichtenberg, J., & Heck, E. (1986). Analysis of sequence and pattern in process research. *Journal of Counseling Psychology, 33,* 170–181.

Light, P., & Glachan, M. (1985). Facilitation of individual problem solving through peer interaction. *Educational Psychology, 5,* 217–255.

Light, P., Littleton, K., Messer, D., & Joiner, R. (1994). Social and communicative processes in computer-based problem solving. *European Journal of Psychology of Education, 9,* 93–109.

Lindow, J. A., & Wilkinson, L. C. (1985). Antecedents and consequences of verbal disagreements during small-group learning. *Journal of Educational Psychology, 77,* 658–667.

Maitland, K., & Goldman, J. (1974). Moral judgment as a function of peer group interaction. *Journal of Personality and Social Psychology, 30,* 699–704.

Martin, L. (1985).The role of social interaction in children's problem solving. *Quarterly Newsletter of the Laboratory of Comparative Human Cognition, 7,* 40–45.

Miller, M. (1987). Argumentation and cognition. In M. Hickmann (Ed.), *Social and functional approaches to language and thought* (pp. 225–250). Orlando, FL: Academic Press.

Miller, P. J. (1994). Narrative practices: Their role in socialization and self construction. In U. Neisser & R. Fivush (Eds.), *The remembered self: Construction and accuracy in the self-narrative.* New York: Cambridge University Press.

Miller, P. M., Danaher, D. L., & Forbes, D. (1986). Sex related strategies for coping with interpersonal conflict in children aged five and seven. *Developmental Psychology, 22,* 543–548.

Miller, S. A. (1981). Conceptions of number. *Genetic Epistemologist, 10,* 1–3.

Miller, S. A., & Brownell, C. (1975). Peers, persuasion, and Piaget: Dyadic interaction between conservers and nonconservers. *Child Development. 46,* 992–997.

Mugny, G., & Doise, W. (1978). Socio-cognitive conflict and structuration of individual and collective performances. *European Journal of Social Psychology, 8,* 181–192.

Nelson, K. (1996). *Language in cognitive development: The emergence of the mediated mind.* New York: Cambridge University Press.

Nicolopoulou, A. (1993). Play, cognitive development, and the social world: Piaget, Vygotsky, and beyond. *Human Development, 36,* 1–23.

Nisan, M. (1976). Delay of gratification in children: Personal versus group choices. *Child Development, 47,* 195–200.

Oyama, S. (1985). *The ontogeny of information: Developmental systems and evolution.* Cambridge, UK: Cambridge University Press.

Pea, R. D. (1982). What is planning development the development of? In D. L. Forbes & M. T. Greenberg (Eds.), *Children's planning strategies.* New Directions in Child Development, No. 18. San Francisco, CA: Jossey-Bass.

Perret-Clermont, A. (1980). *Social interaction and cognitive development in children.* European Monographs in Social Psychology. London: Academic Press.

Peterson, C. C., & Peterson, J. L. (1990). Sociocognitive conflict and spatial perspective-taking in deaf children. *Journal of Applied Developmental Psychology, 11,* 267–281.

Piaget, J. (1934). *The moral judgment of the child.* London: Routledge & Kegan Paul.

Piaget, J. (1950). *The psychology of intelligence.* London: Routledge & Kegan Paul.

Piaget, J. (1962). *Play, dreams, and imitation in childhood.* New York: Norton.

Piaget, J. (1967). *The language and thought of the child.* London: Routledge & Kegan Paul.

Piaget, J. (1971). *Psychology and epistemology.* New York: Grossman.

Piaget, J. (1985). *The equilibration of cognitive structures.* Chicago: University of Chicago Press.

Piaget, J. (1995). *Sociological studies.* London: Routledge.

Radziszewska, B., & Rogoff, B. (1991). Children's guided participation in planning imaginary errands with skilled adult or peer partners. *Developmental Psychology, 27,* 381–389.

Rogoff, B. (1990). *Apprenticeship in thinking: Cognitive development in social context.* Oxford, UK: Oxford University Press.

Rogoff, B. (1998). Cognition as a collaborative process. In W. Damon (Gen. Ed.) & D. Kuhn & R. S. Siegler (Eds.), *Handbook of child psychology: Vol. 2. Cognition, perception and language,* (pp. 679–744). New York: Wiley.

Rogoff, B., & Gauvain, M. (1986). A method for the analysis of patterns, illustrated with data on mother-child instructional interaction. In J. Valsiner (Ed.), *The individual subject and scientific psychology* (pp. 261–290). New York: Plenum.

Rogoff, B., Gauvain, M., & Ellis, S. (1984). Development viewed in its cultural context. In M. H. Bornstein & M. E. Lamb (Eds.), *Developmental psychology: An advanced textbook* (pp. 533–571). Hillsdale, NJ: Erlbaum.

Rommetveit, R. (1976). On Piagetian cognitive operations, semantic competence and message structure in adult-child communication. In I. Markova (Ed.), *The social context of language.* London: Wiley.

Rubin, K. H., Bukowski, W., & Parker, J. G. (1998). Peer interactions, relationships, and groups. In B. Damon (Gen. Ed.) N. Eisenberg (Ed.), *Handbook of child psychology: Vol. 3, So-*

cial, emotional, and personality development (pp. 619–700). New York: Wiley.

Rubin, K. H., Fein, G. A., & Vandenberg, B. (1983). Play. In P. H. Mussen (Series Ed.) & E. M. Hetherington (Ed.), *Handbook of child psychology: Vol. 4, Socialization, personality and social development* (pp. 693–774). New York: Wiley.

Sachs, J. (1987). Preschool boys' and girls' language use in pretend play. In S. U. Phillips, S. Steele, & C. Tanz (Eds.), *Language, gender, and sex in comparative perspective* (pp. 178–188). Cambridge: Cambridge University Press.

Saxe, G. (1994). *Culture and cognitive development: Studies in mathematical understanding.* Hillsdale, NJ: Erlbaum.

Schafer, R. (1968). *Aspects of internalization.* New York: International Universities Press.

Scribner, S. (1985). Thinking in action: Some characteristics of practical thought. In R. J. Sternberg & R. K. Wagner (Eds.), *Practical intelligence: Origins of competence in the everyday world.* New York: Cambridge University Press.

Selman, R. L. (1980). *The growth of interpersonal understanding.* New York: Academic Press.

Selman, R. L., & Jaquette, D. (1977). *The development of interpersonal awareness.* Unpublished manuscript, Harvard University.

Selman, R. L., & Schultz, L. (1988). Children's strategies for interpersonal negotiation with peers: An interpretive/empirical approach to the study of social development. In T. J. Berndt & G. W. Ladd (Eds.), *Peer relationships in childhood.* New York: Wiley.

Shantz, C. U., (1987). Conflicts between children. *Child Development, 58,* 283–305.

Shantz, C. U., & Hartup W. W. (Eds). (1992). *Conflict in child and adolescent development.* New York: Cambridge University Press.

Sheldon, A. (1990). Pickle fights: Gendered talk in preschool disputes. *Discourse Processes, 13,* 5–31.

Siegler, R. S. (1981). Developmental sequences within and between concepts. *Monographs of the Society for Research in Child Development, 46,* 1–74.

Sigel, I. E. (1993). The centrality of a distancing model for the development of representational competence. In R. Cocking & A. Renninger (Eds.), *The development and meaning of psychological distance* (pp. 141–160). Hillsdale, NJ: Erlbaum.

Silverman, I., & Geiringer, E. (1973). Dyadic interaction and conservation induction: A test of Piaget's equilibration model. *Child Development, 44,* 815–820.

Smedslund, J. (1966). Les origenes sociales de la decentration. In F. Bresson & H. de Montmollin (Eds.), *Psychologie et epistemologie genetiques: Themes Piagetiens.* Paris: Dunod.

Stetsenko, A. (1999). Social interaction, cultural tools, and the zone of proximal development: In search of a synthesis. In M. Hedgaard, S. Chaiklin, S. Boedker, & U. J. Jensen (Eds.), *Activity, theory and social practice. Proceedings of the ISCRAT 1998: Keynote speeches and panels* (pp. 235–253). Aarhus, Denmark: Aarhus University Press.

Stetsenko, A., & Arievitch, I. (1997). Constructing and deconstructing the self: Comparing post-Vygotskian and discourse-based versions of social constructivism. *Mind, Culture, and Activity, 4,* 159–172.

Thelen, E., & Smith, L. B. (1994). *A dynamic systems approach to development: Applications.* Cambridge, MA: MIT Press.

Thelen, E., & Smith, L. B. (1998). Dynamic systems theory. In W. Damon (Gen. Ed.) & R. Lerner (Ed.), *Handbook of child psychology: Vol. 1: Theoretical models of human development* (pp. 563–634). New York: Wiley.

Tomasello, M. (1998). Social cognition and the evolution of culture. In J. Langer & M. Killen (Eds.), *Piaget, evolution and development.* Mahwah, NJ: Erlbaum.

Tryphon, A., & Voneche, J. (1996). *Piaget-Vygotsky: The social genesis of thought.* East Sussex, UK: Psychology Press.

Tudge, J. (1985). The effect of social interaction on cognitive development: How creative is conflict? *Quarterly News-*

letter of the Laboratory of Comparative Human Cognition, 7, 33–40.

Tudge, J. (1992). Processes and consequences of peer collaboration: A Vygotskian analysis. *Child Development, 63,* 1364–1379.

Tudge, J., & Rogoff, B. (1989). Peer influences on cognitive development: Piagetian and Vygotskian perspectives. In M. Bornstein & J. Bruner (Eds.), *Interaction in human development* (pp. 17– 40). Hillsdale, NJ: Erlbaum.

Valsiner, J., & Cairns, R. B. (1992). Theoretical perspectives on conflict and development. In C. U. Shantz & W. Hartup (Eds.), *Conflict in child and adolescent development* (pp. 15–35). Cambridge: Cambridge University Press.

van der Veer, R. (1996). Vygotsky and Piaget: A collective monologue. *Human Development, 39,* 237–242.

van Dijk, T. (Ed.). (1985). *Handbook of discourse analysis.* London: Academic Press.

Verba, M. (1994).The beginnings of collaboration in peer interaction. *Human Development, 37,* 125–139.

Verba, M., & Winnykamen, F. (1992). Expert-novice interactions: Influence of partner status. *European Journal of Psychology of Education, 7,* 61–71.

Vygotsky, L. S. (1962). *Thought and language.* Cambridge, MA: M.I.T. Press.

Vygotsky, L. S. (1967). Play and its role in the mental development of the child. *Soviet Psychology, 5,* 6–18.

Vygotsky, L. S. (1978). *Mind in society: The development of higher psychological processes.* Cambridge, MA: Harvard University Press.

Vygotsky, L. S. (1981). The genesis of higher mental functions. In J. V. Wertsch (Ed.), *The concept of activity in Soviet psychology* (pp. 134–143). Armonk, NY: M. E. Sharpe.

Vygotsky, L. S. (1987). The problem of speech and thinking in Piaget's theory. In R. W. Reiber & A. S. Carton (Eds.), *The collected works of L. S. Vygotsky: Vol. 1. Problems of general psychology* (pp. 53–91). New York: Plenum.

References

Walker, L. (1983). Sources of cognitive conflict for stage transition in moral development. *Developmental Psychology, 19,* 103–110.

Wartofsky, M. (1983). The child's construction of the world and the world's construction of the child: From historical epistemology to historical psychology. In F. S. Kessen & A. W. Sigel (Eds.), *The child and other cultural inventions* (pp. 188–233). New York: Praeger.

Webb, N. M. (1984). Sex differences in interaction and achievement in cooperative small groups. *Journal of Educational Psychology, 76,* 33–44.

Weinstein, B., & Bearison, D. J. (1984). Social interaction, social observation and cognitive development in young children. *European Journal of Social Psychology, 15,* 333–343.

Werner, H. (1937). Process and achievement: A basic problem of education and developmental psychology. *Harvard Educational Review, 7,* 353–368.

Werner, H. (1948). *Comparative psychology of mental development.* New York: International Universities Press.

Wertsch, J. V. (1979). *The concept of activity in Soviet psychology.* Armonk, NY: Sharpe.

Wertsch, J. V. (1991). *Voices of the mind: A sociocultural approach to mediated action.* Cambridge, MA: Harvard University Press.

Wertsch, J. V. (1993). Commentary on: Conceptual roots of internalization: From transmission to transformation. *Human Development, 36,* 168–171.

Wertsch, J. V. (1998). *Mind as action.* New York: Oxford University Press.

Wertsch, J. V., & Bivens, J. A. (1993). The social origins of individual mental functioning: Alternatives and perspectives. In R. Cocking & A. Renninger (Eds.), *The development and meaning of psychological distance* (pp. 203–218). Hillsdale, NJ: Erlbaum.

Wilkinson, L. C. & Marrett, C. B. (Eds.). (1985). *Gender influences in the classroom.* Orlando, FL: Academic Press.

Index

About the Authors and Contributors

David J. Bearison is Professor of Psychology in the Doctoral Programs in Developmental Psychology, Educational Psychology, and Health Psychology at the Graduate School and University Center of the City University of New York, and Adjunct Professor of Pediatrics at the Mount Sinai School of Medicine. He is the author of *They Never Want to Tell You—Children Talk About Cancer* and the co-editor of *Pediatric Psychooncology.*

Bruce Dorval is a Visiting Scholar in Developmental Psychology at the Graduate School and University Center of the City of New York and is in private practice in Manhattan. He is a Candidate at the Institute for Psychoanalytic Training and Research in New York City and the editor of *Conversational Organization and its Development.*

Anna Stetsenko first studied and then worked (1975 until 1990) at the Psychology Department of the Moscow State University which was, at the time, the hotbed of Vygotsky, Leont'ev, and Luria's cultural-historical activity theory. Today, she advances

activity theory as Professor of Psychology and Head of the Ph.D.
Program in Developmental Psychology at the Graduate Center
of the City University of New York.

Gess LeBlanc, Daniela Plesa, and **Andrea Sadow** were doctoral
candidates in the Ph.D. Program in Developmental Psychology
at the Graduate Center of the City University of New York and
Research Associates in the present study of children's collaborative cognition. Dr. LeBlanc presently is Assistant Professor at
Hunter College of the City University of New York. Dr. Plesa is
Research Coordinator in the Laboratory of Developmental Cognitive Neuroscience at Boston University Medical School and Ms.
Sadow has left the field to pursue other interests.